I0409386

I'm ExtraOrdinary

Your Author
BTArtist

I'm

Extra.

oRdiNaRy

Your Author
BTArtist

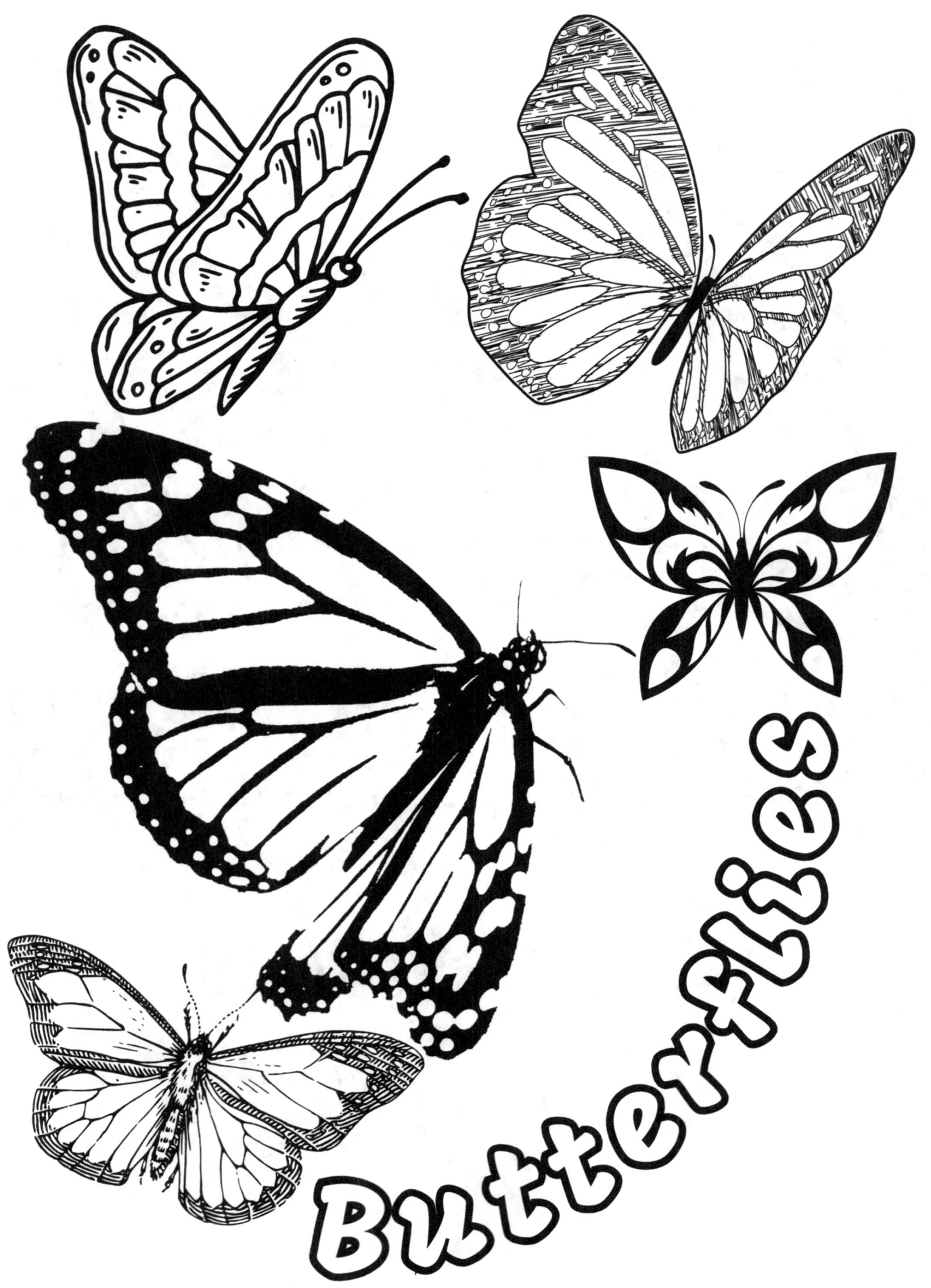

Butterflies

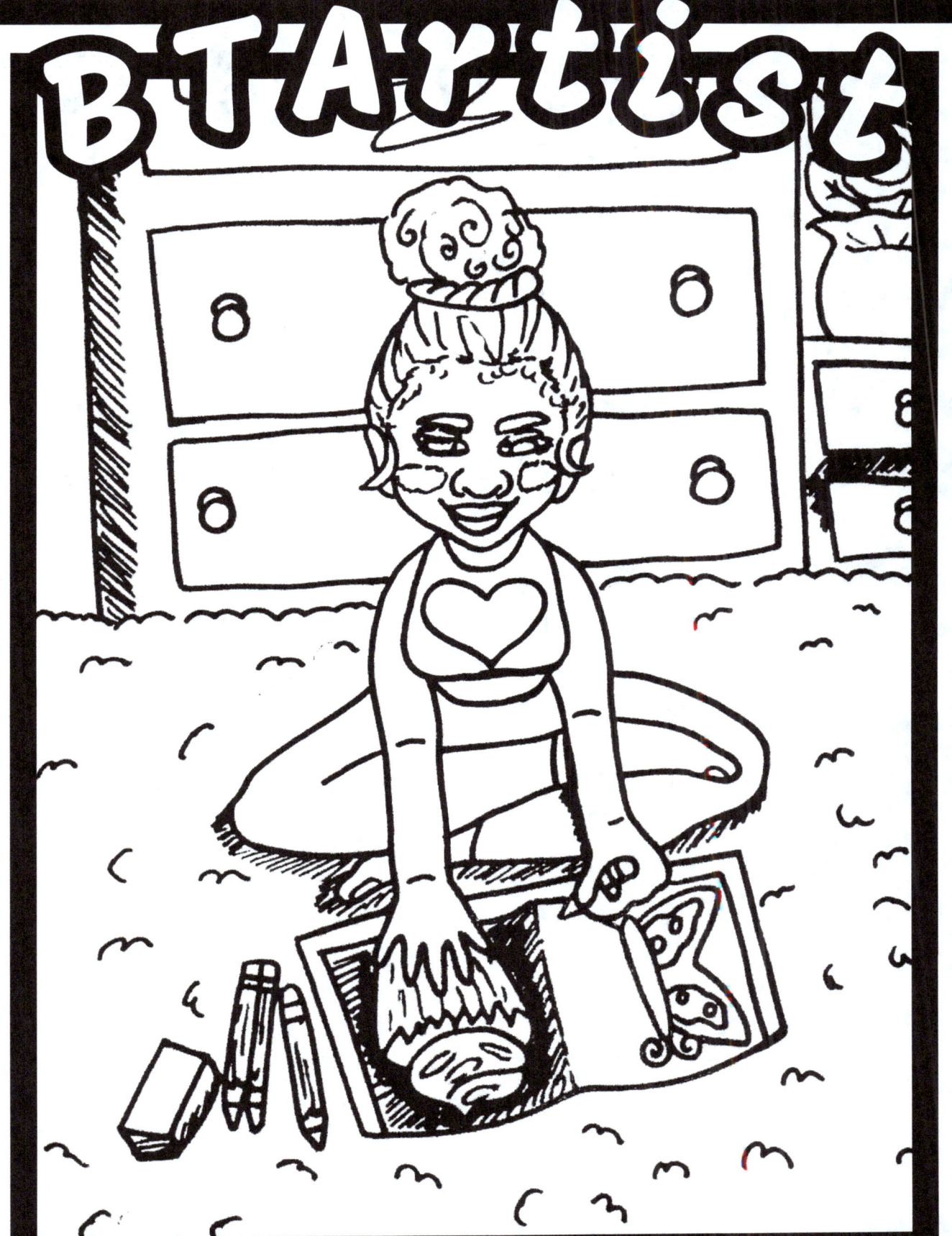

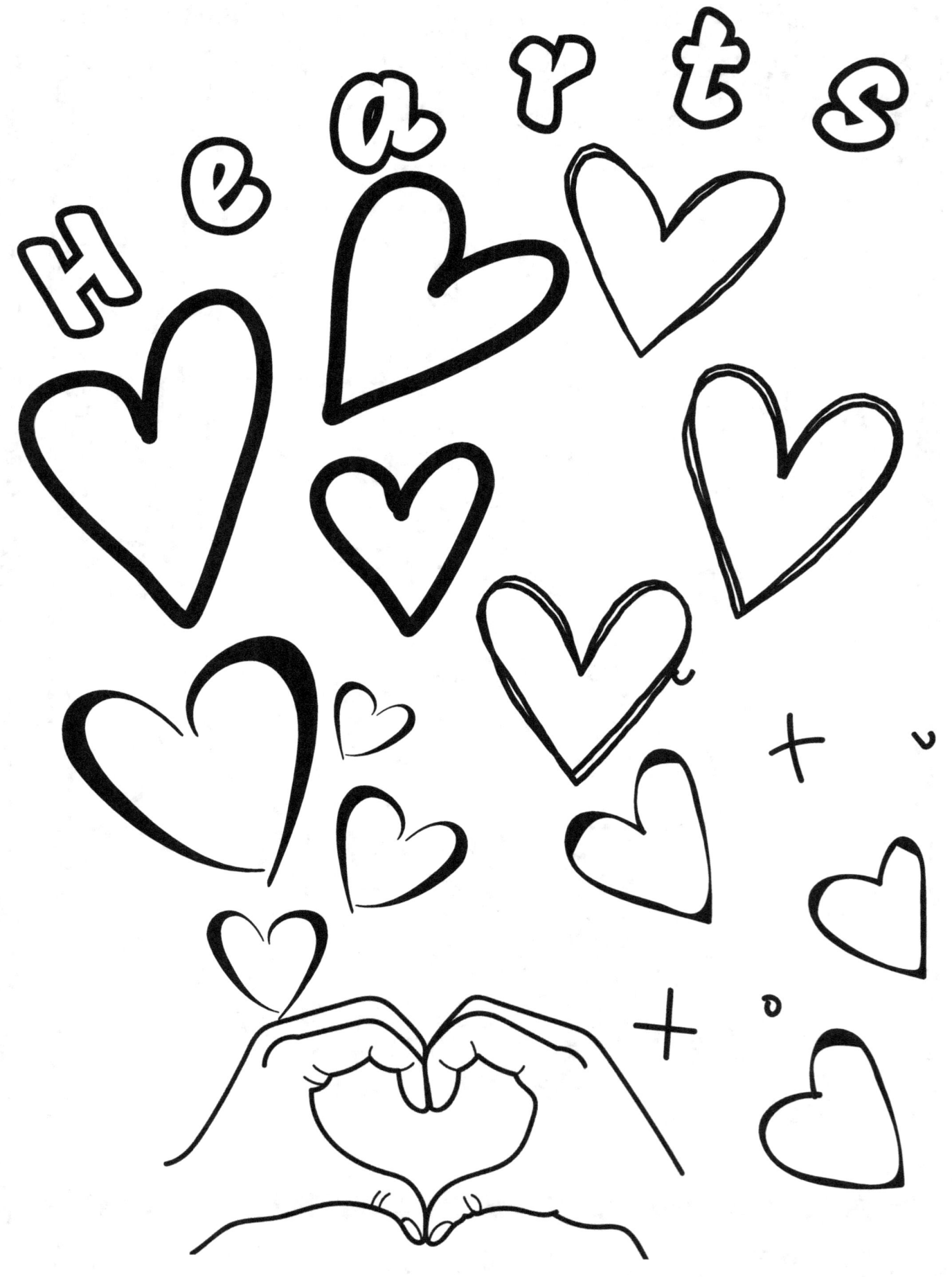

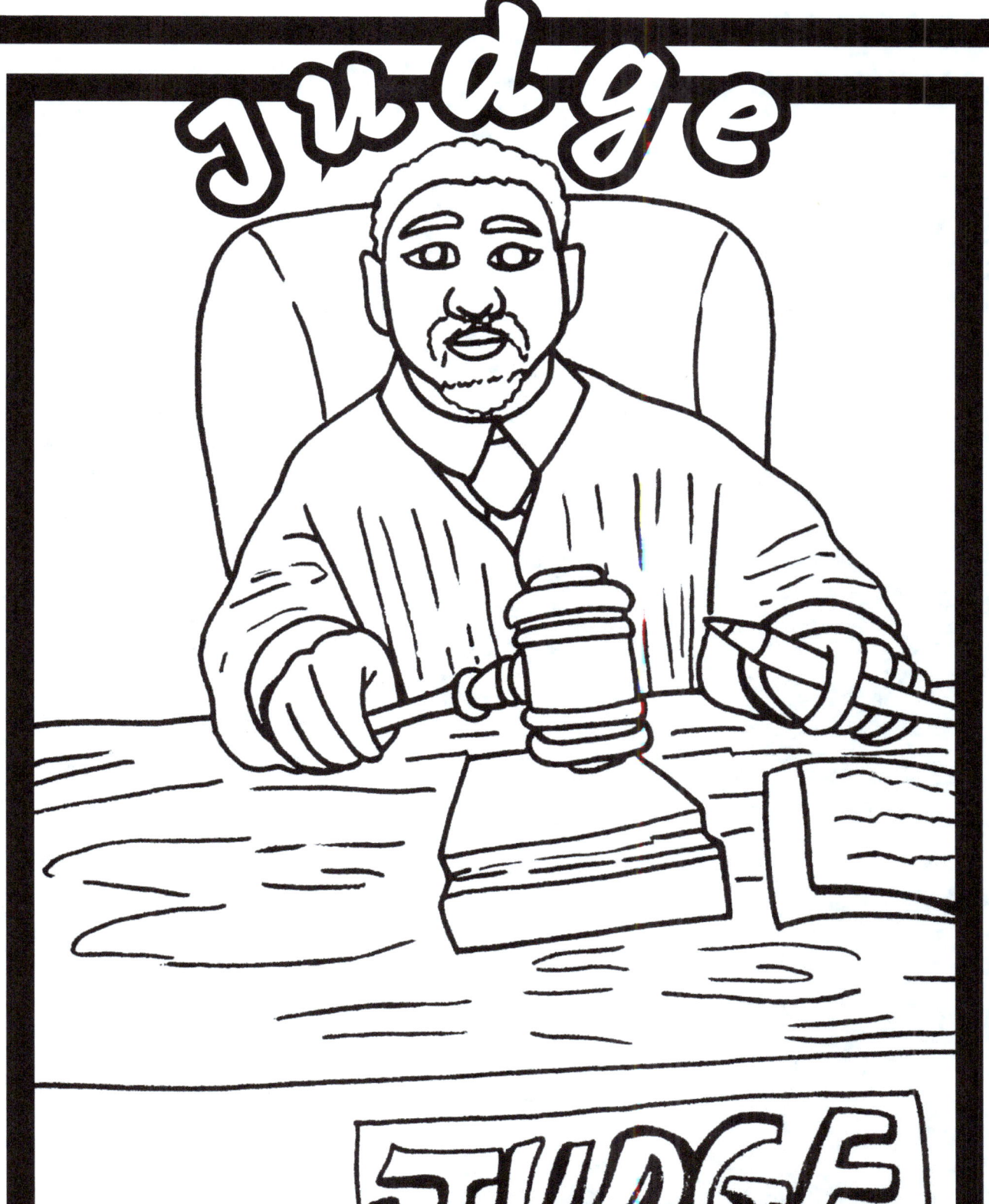

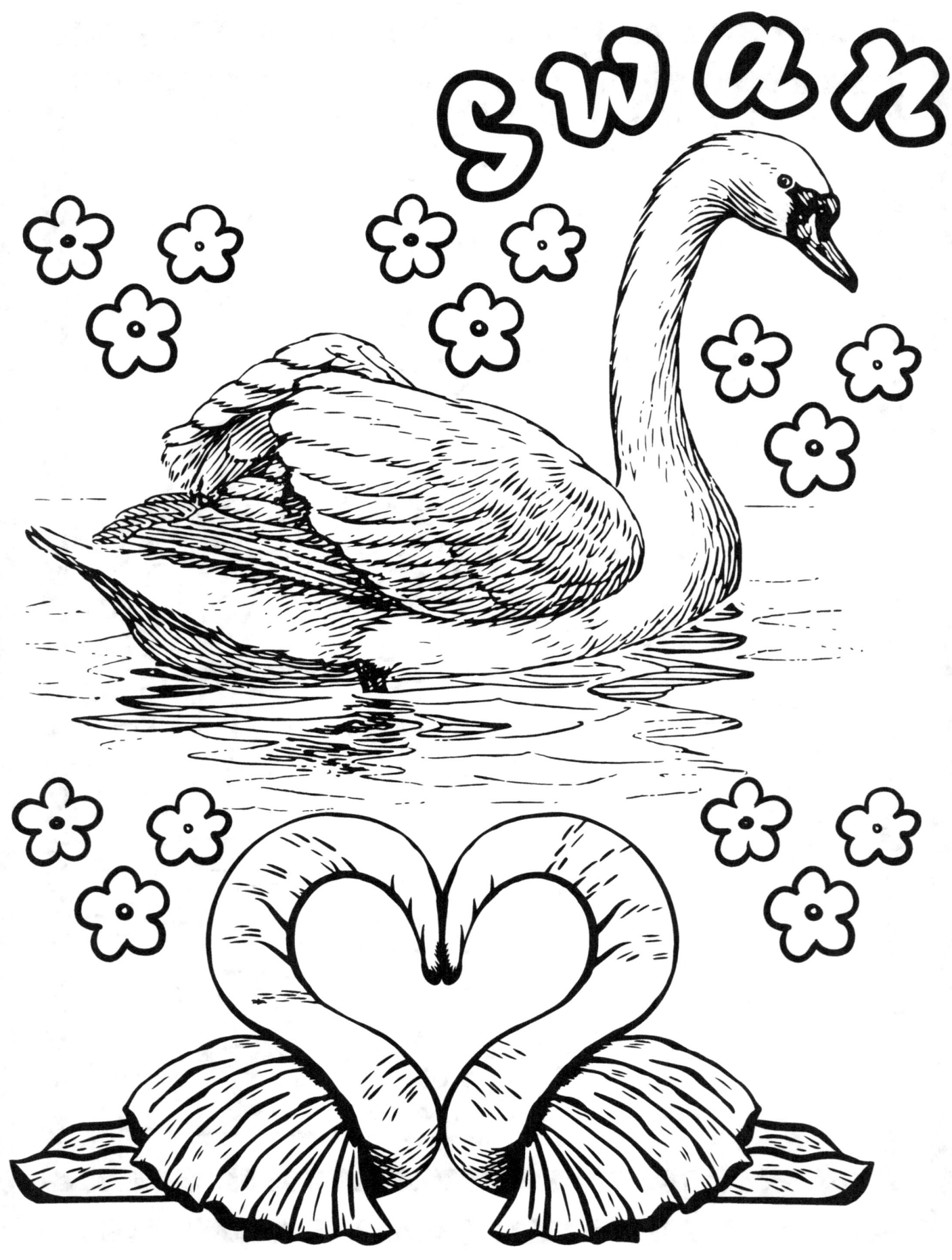

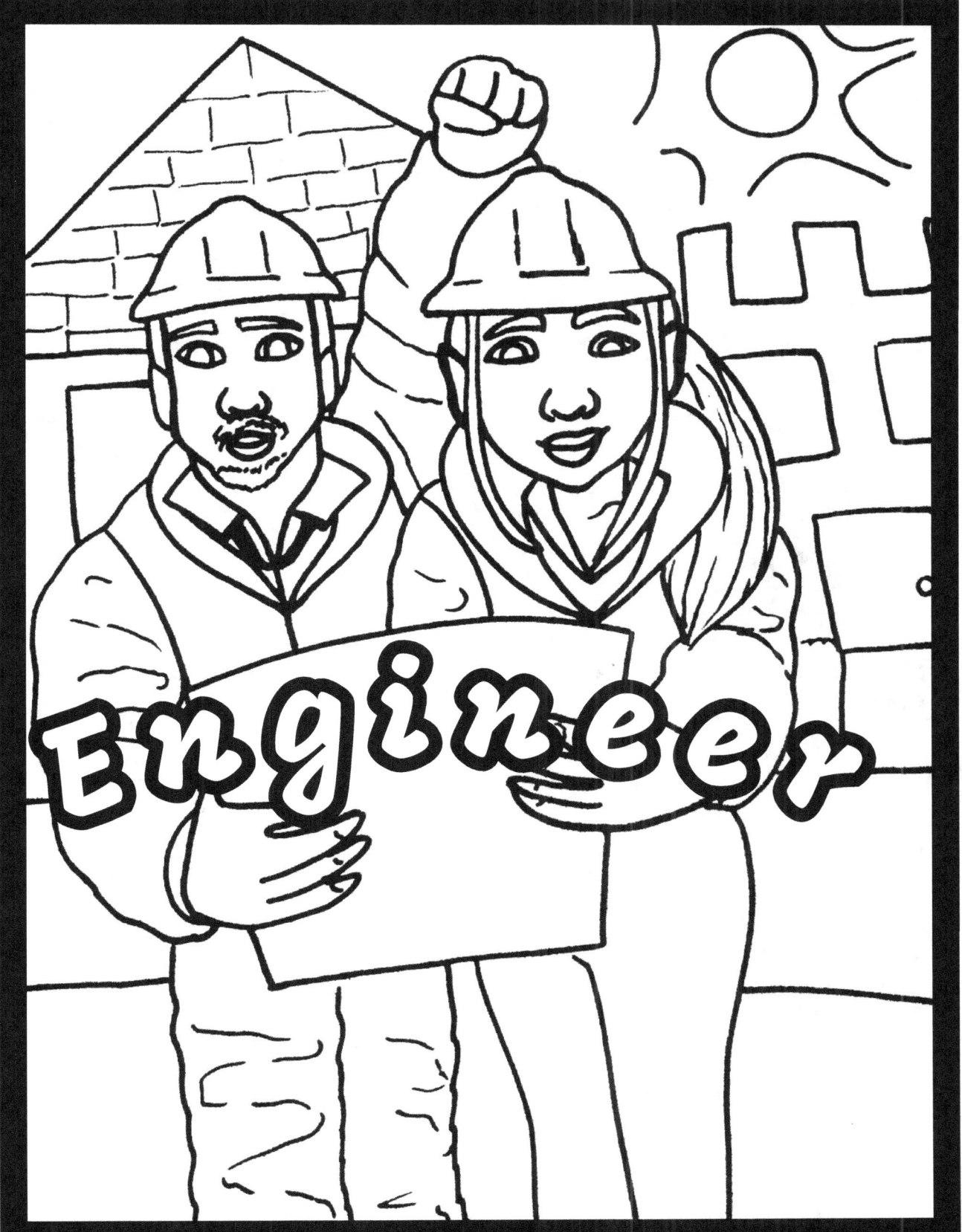

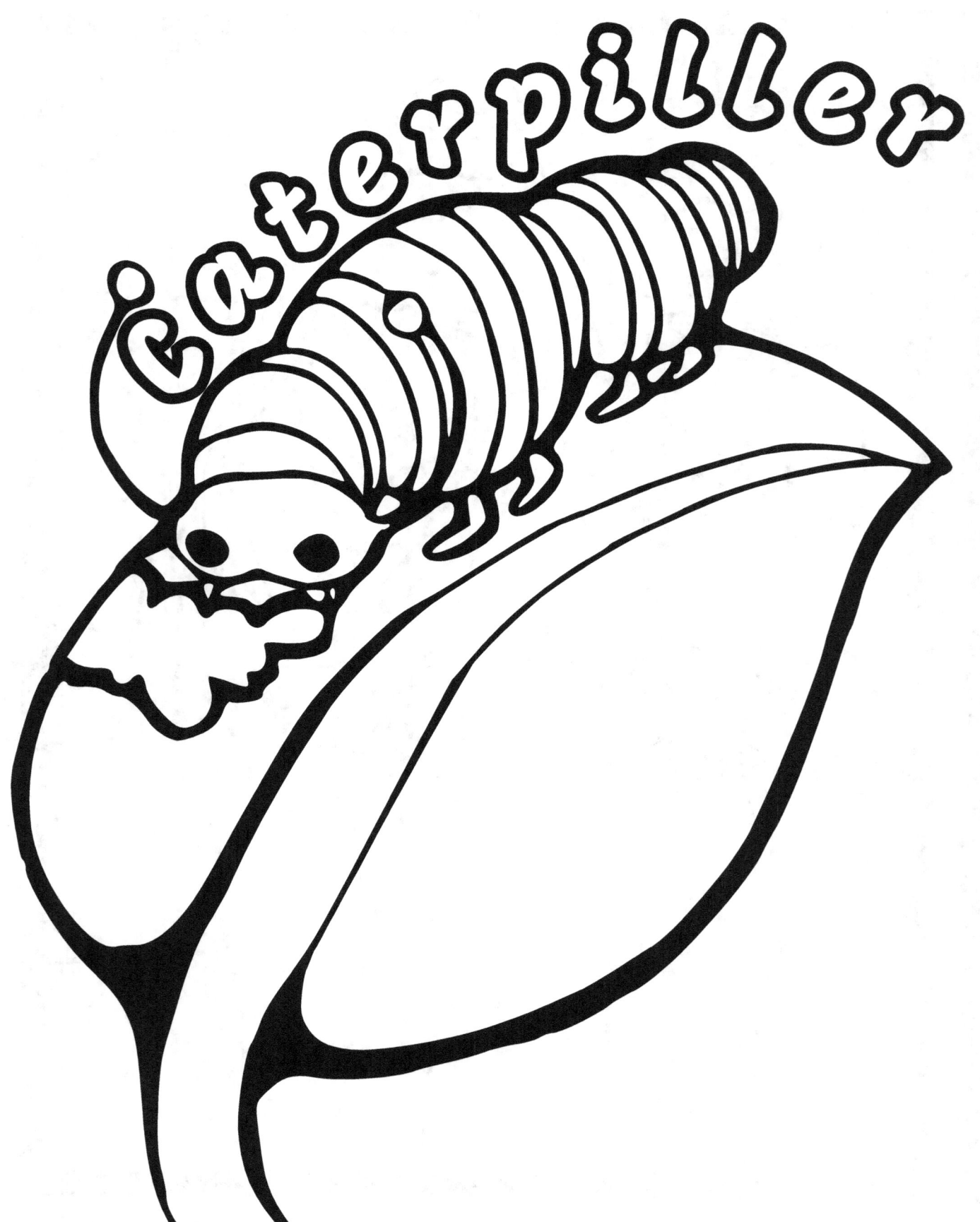

Caterpiller

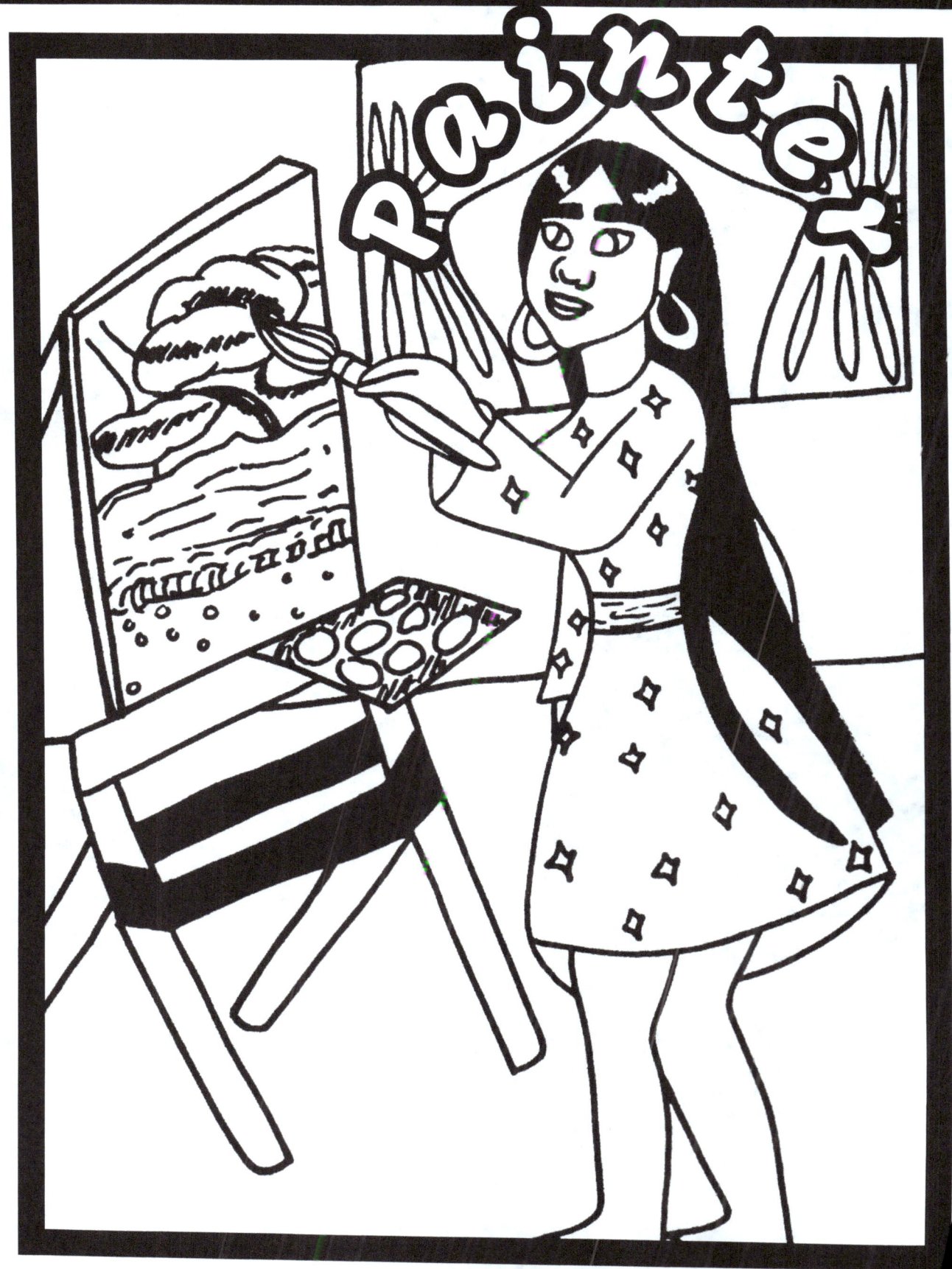

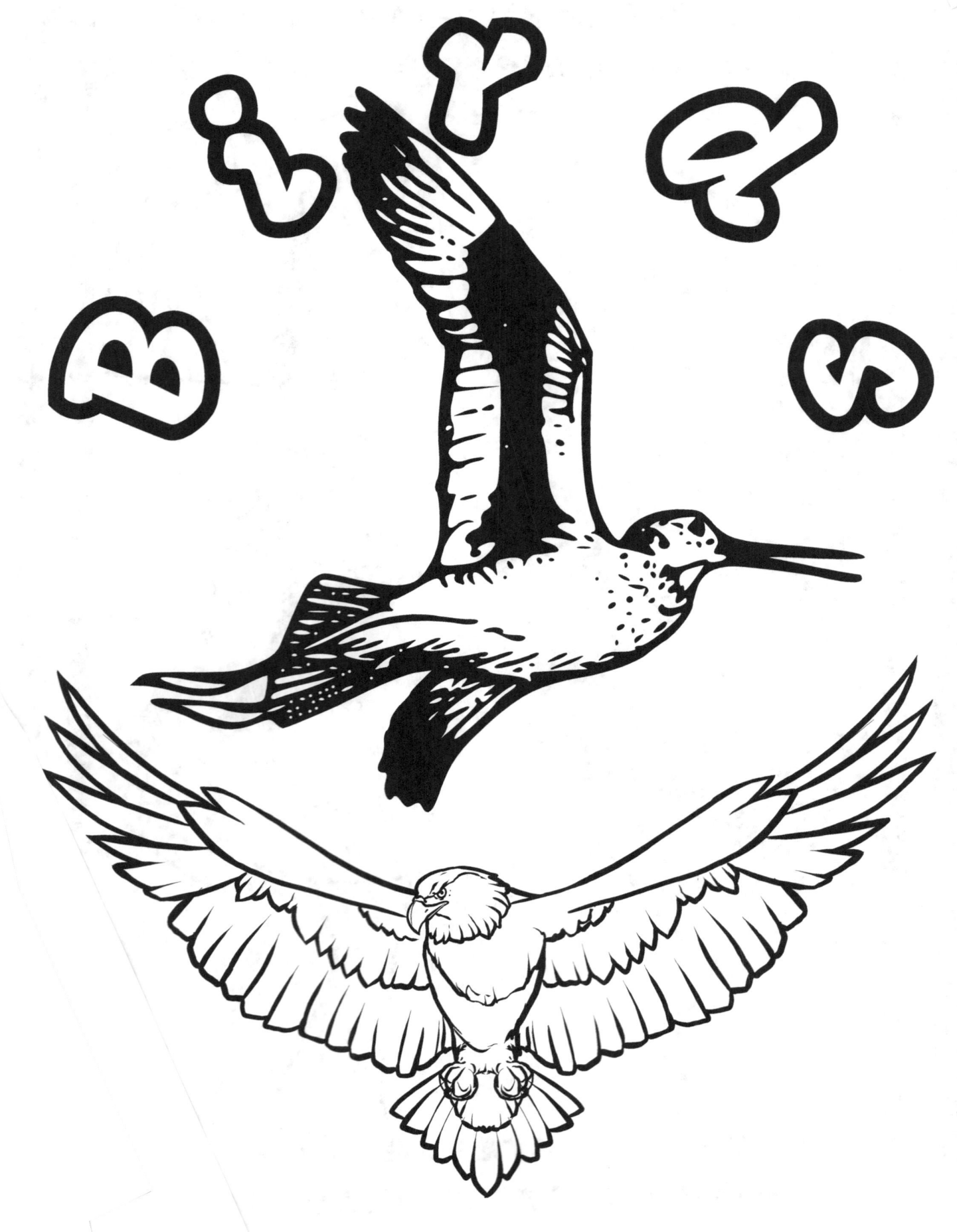

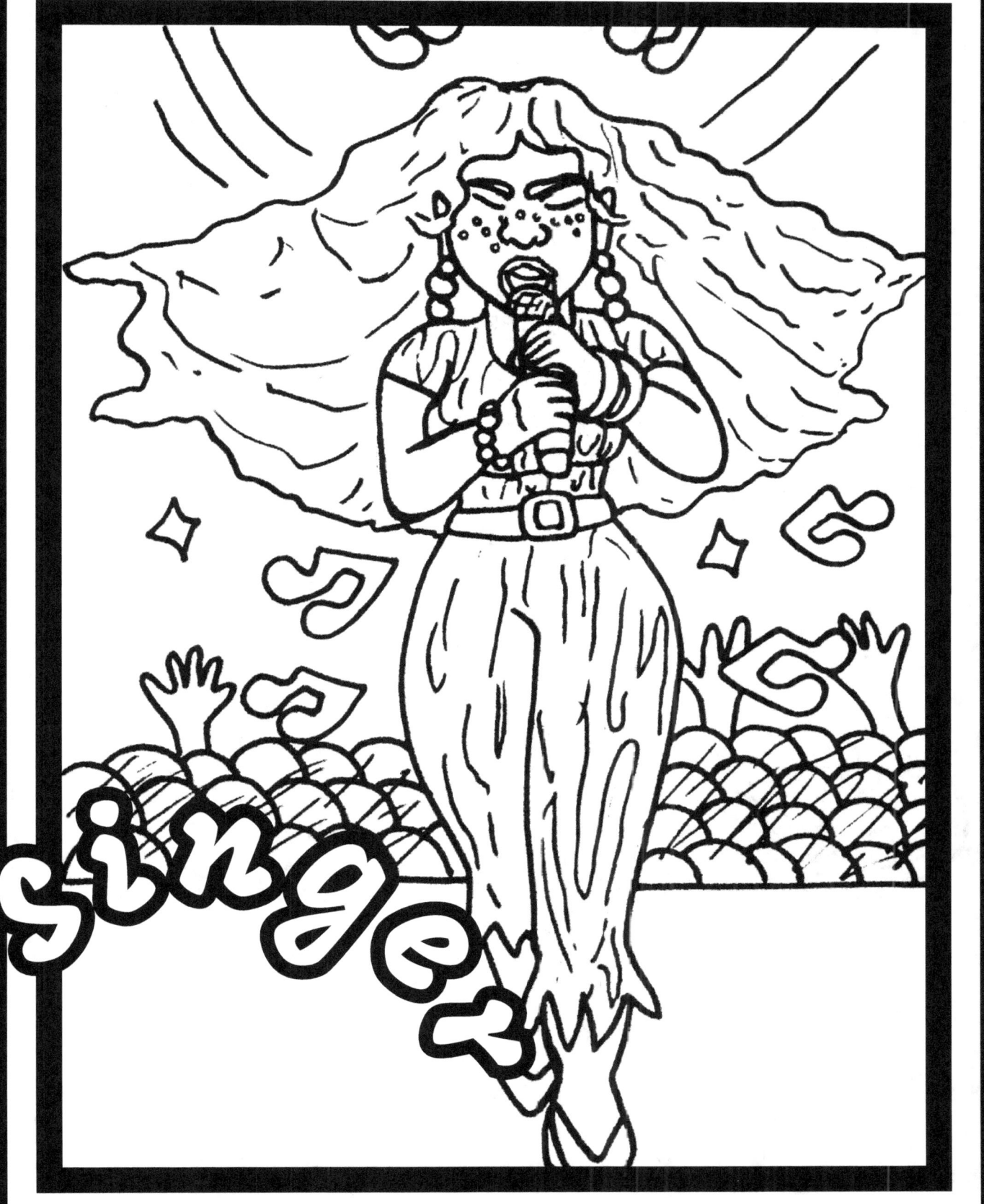

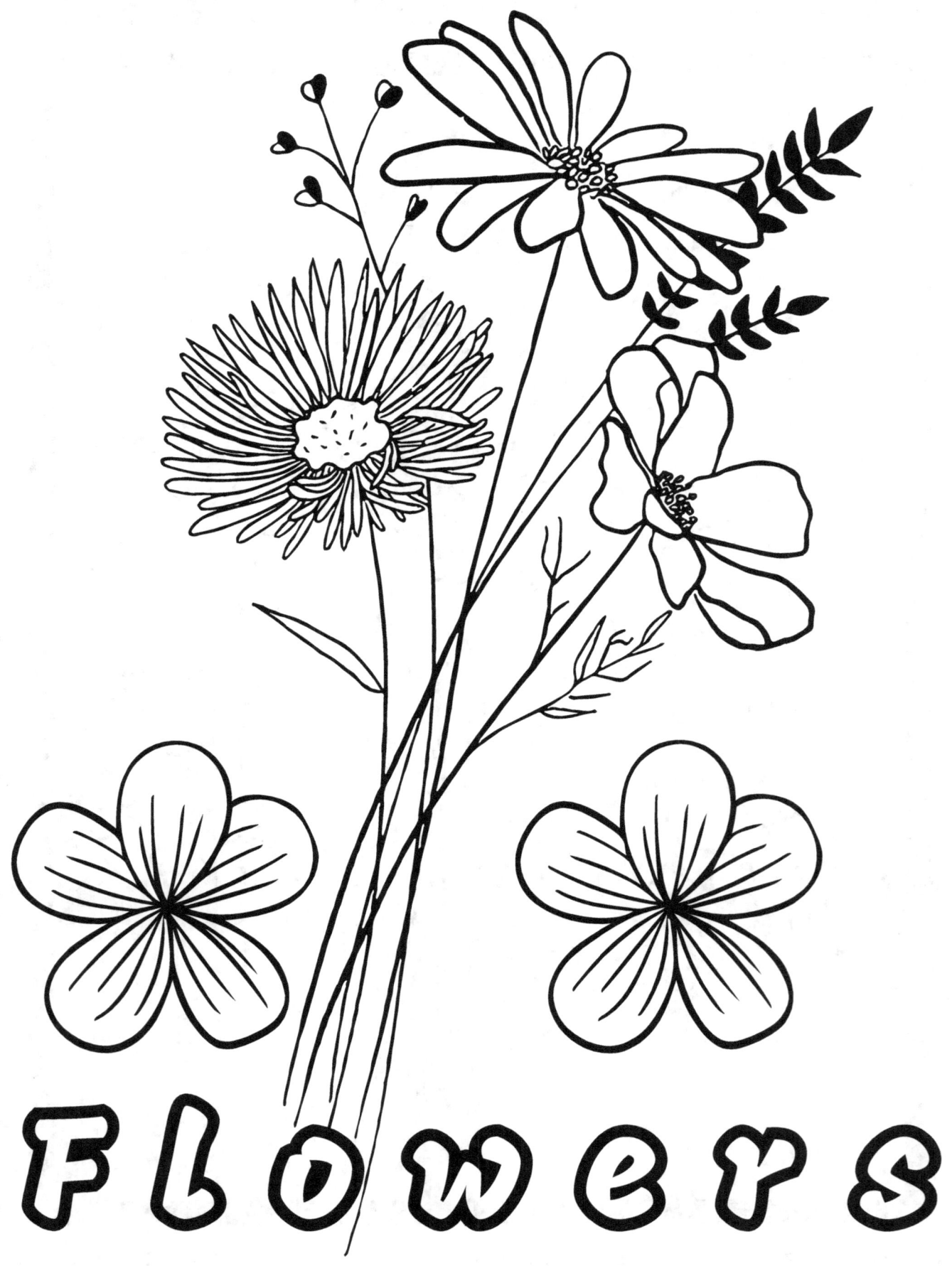

Flowers

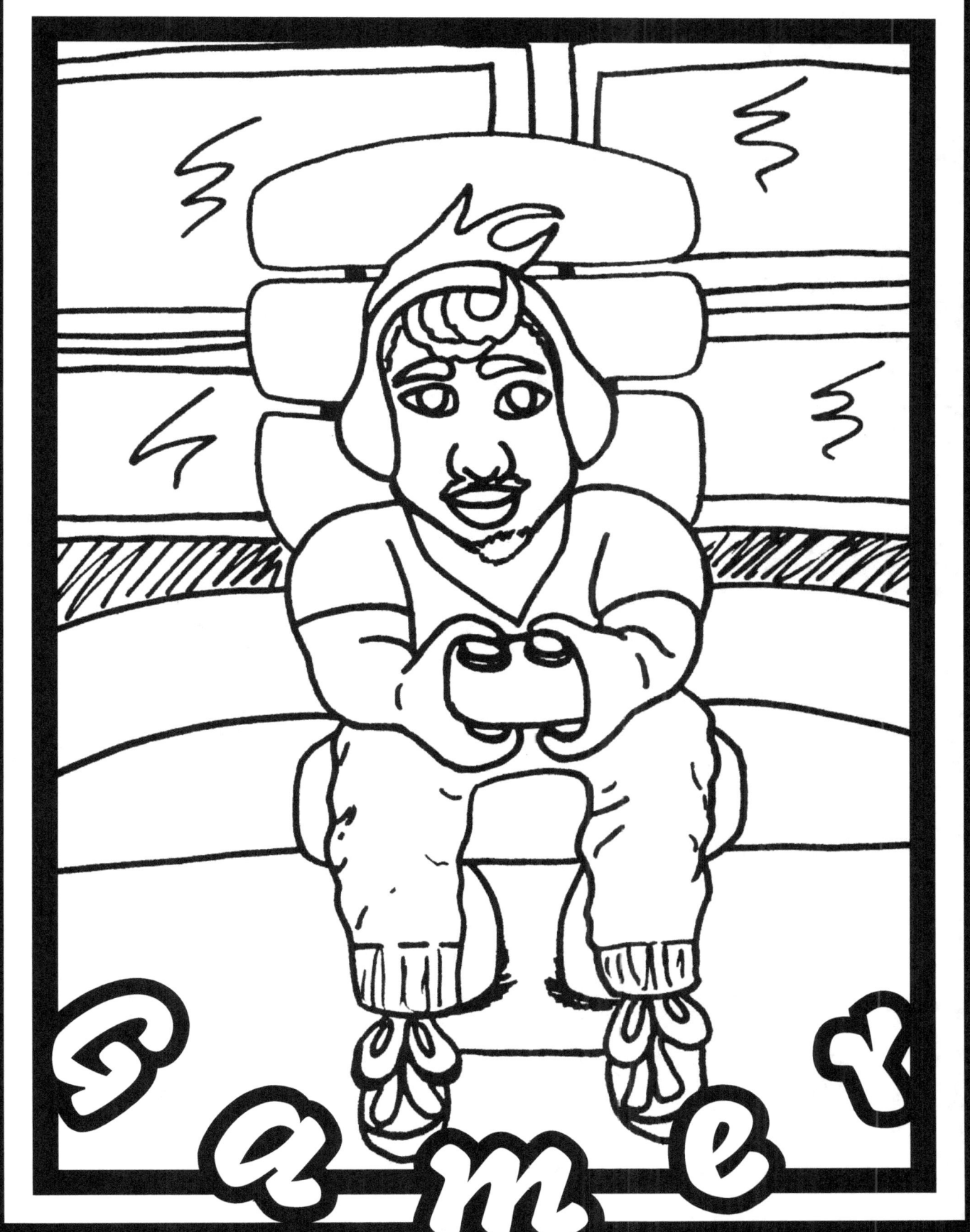

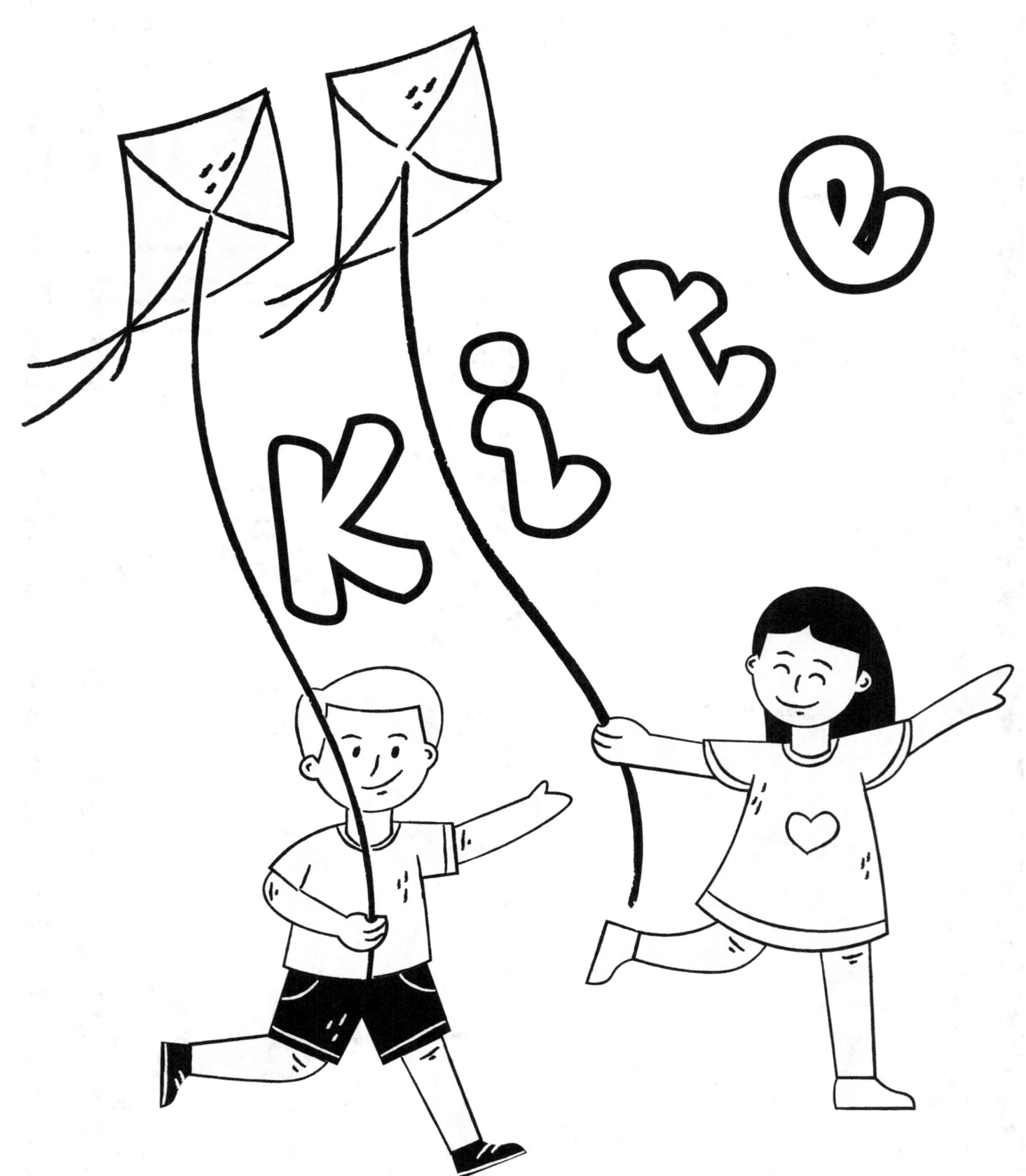

Liberian

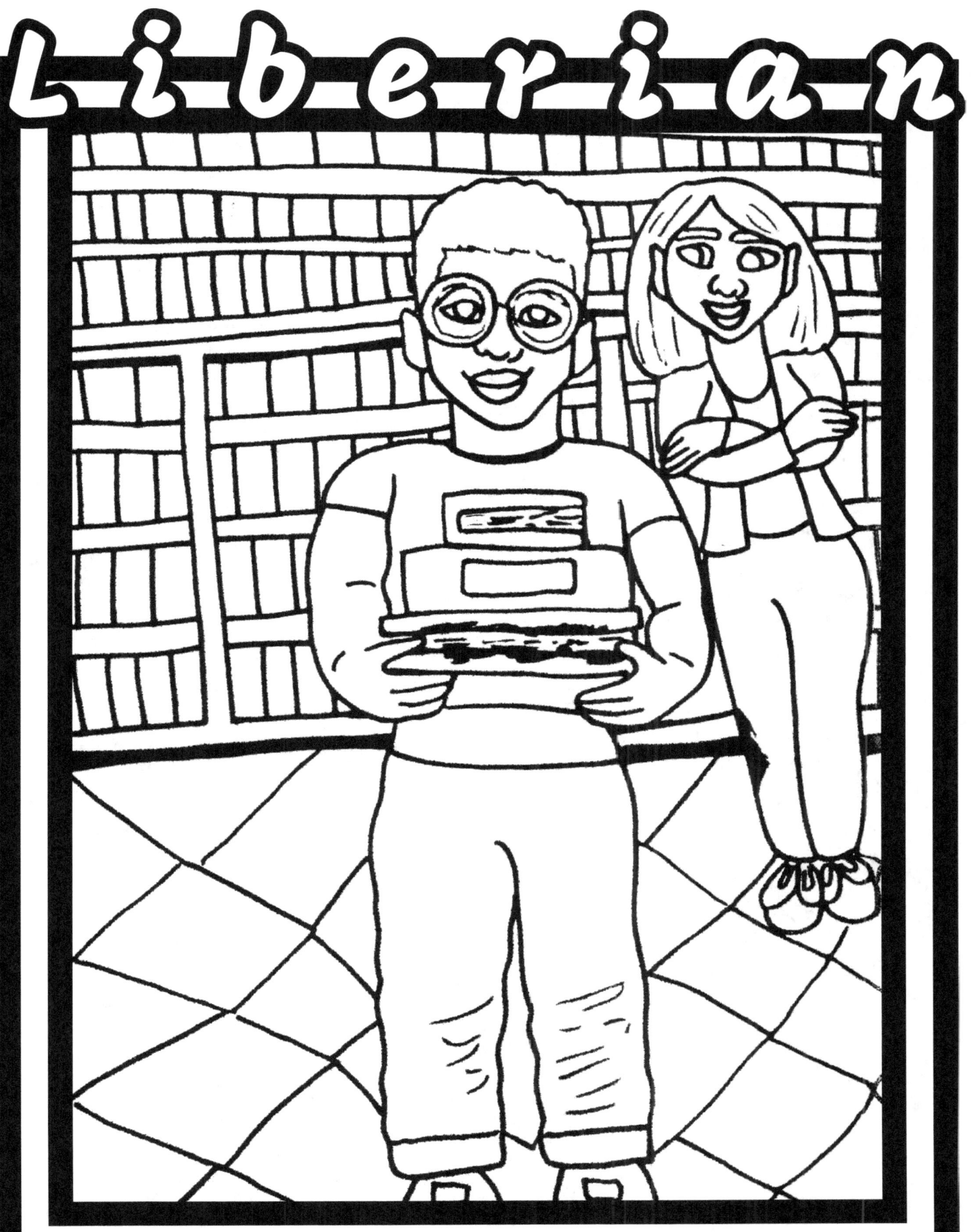

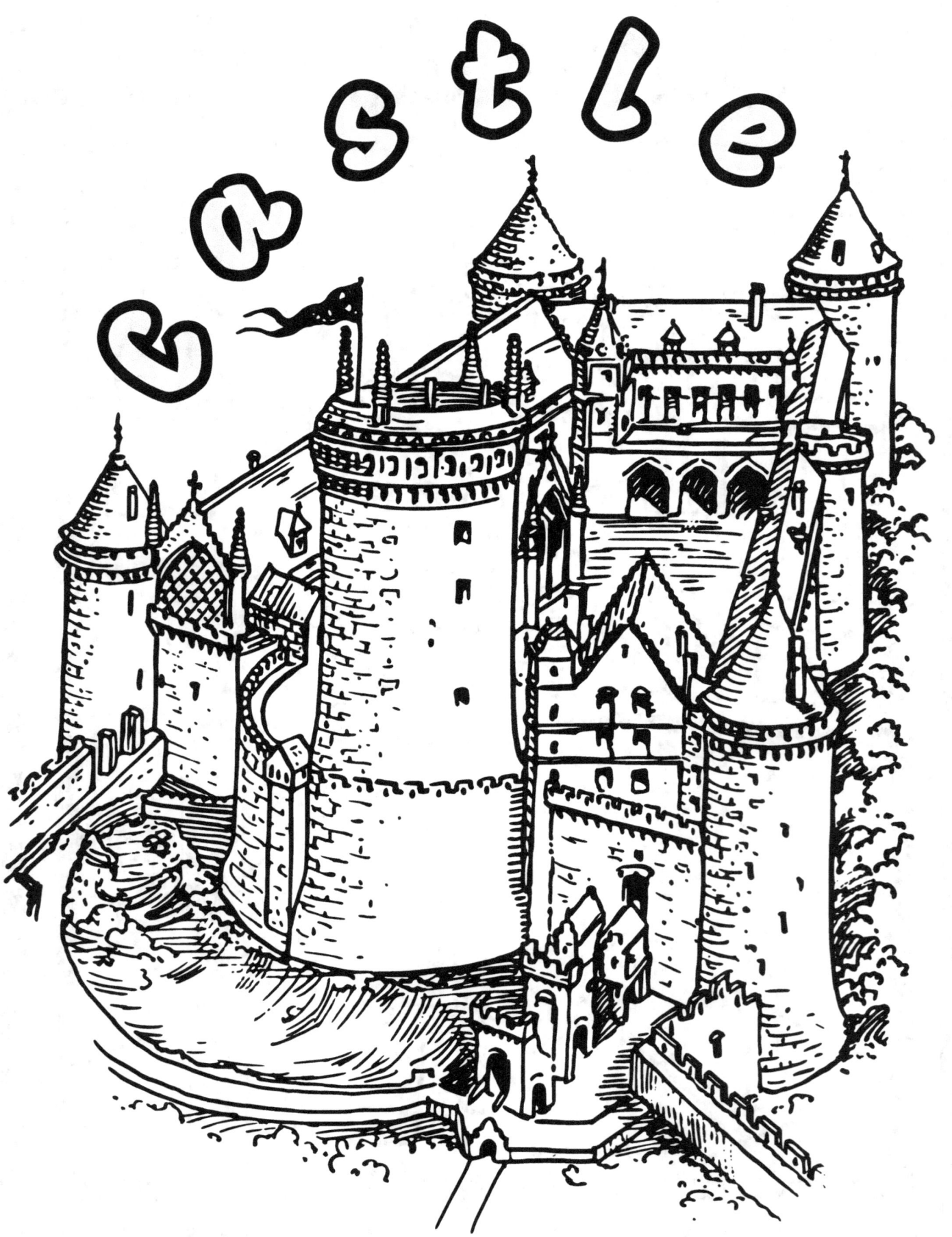

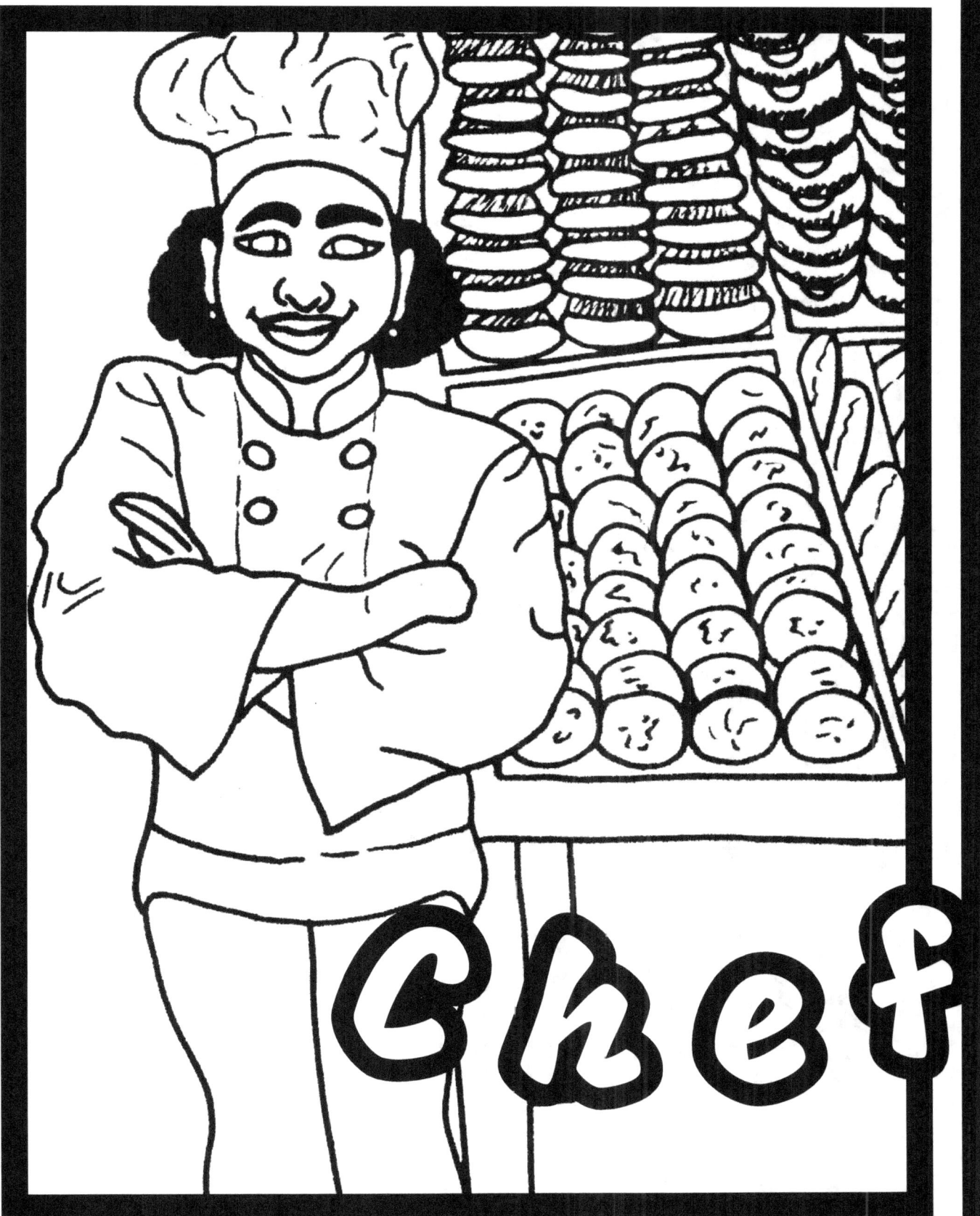

Chef

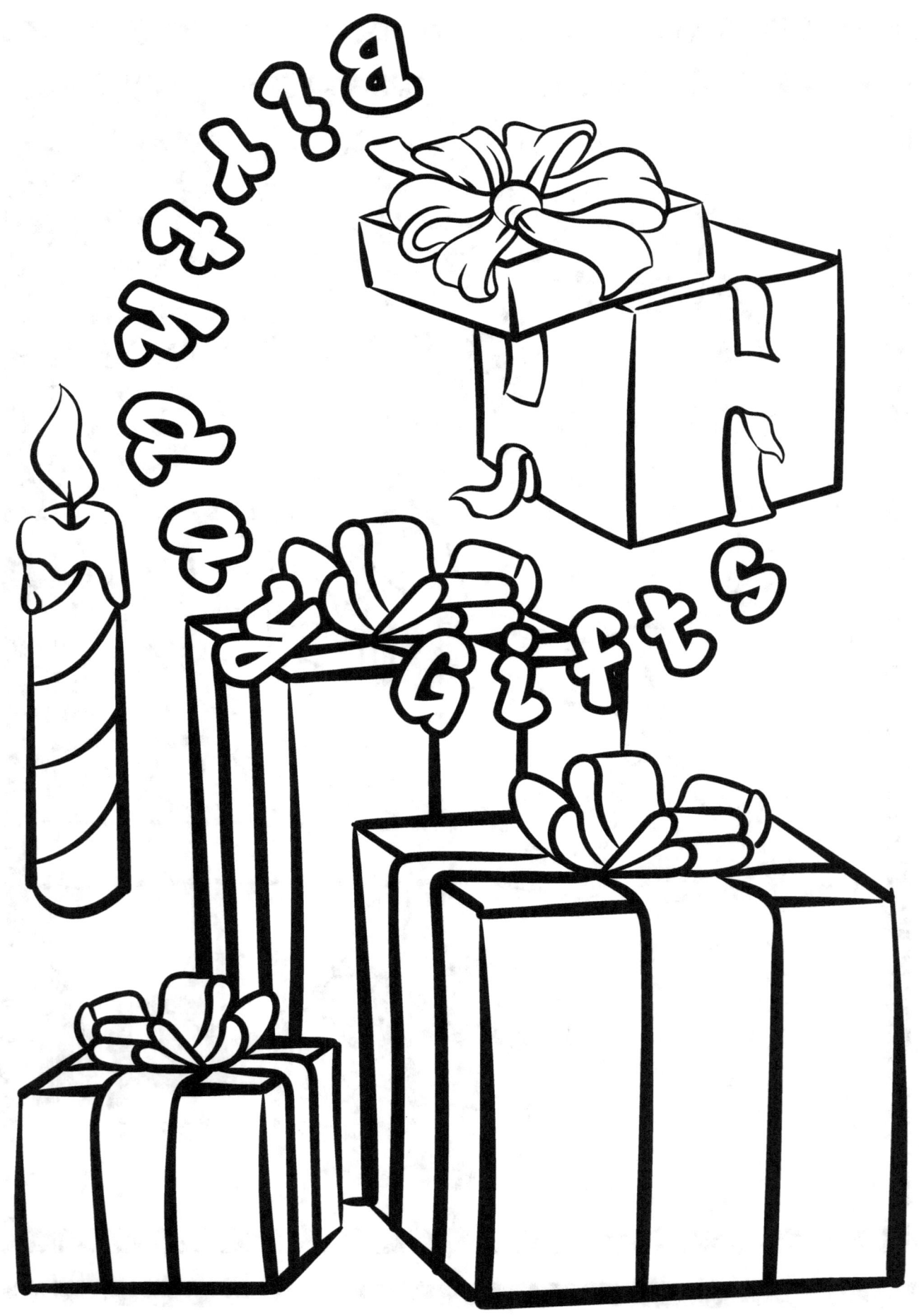

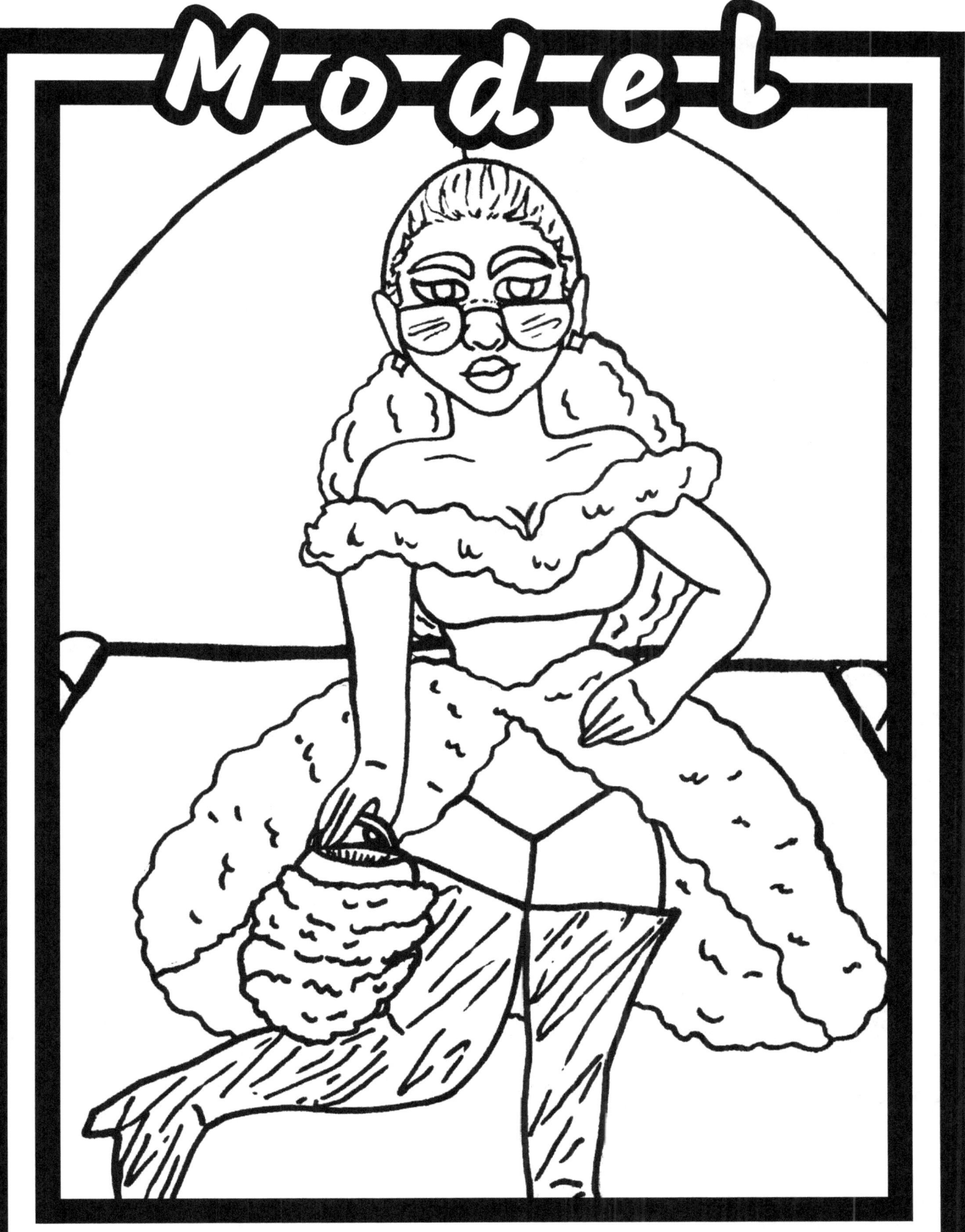

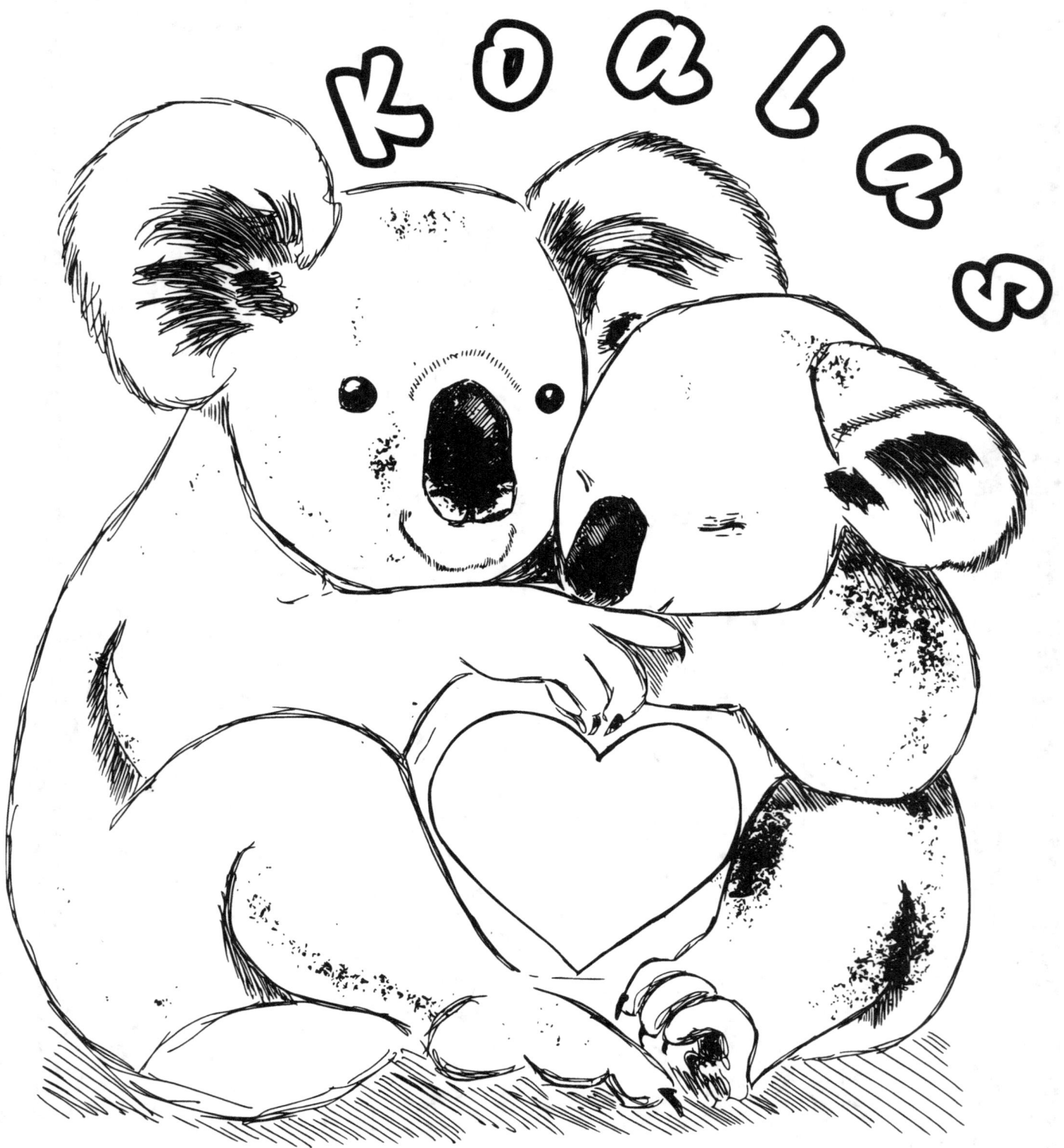

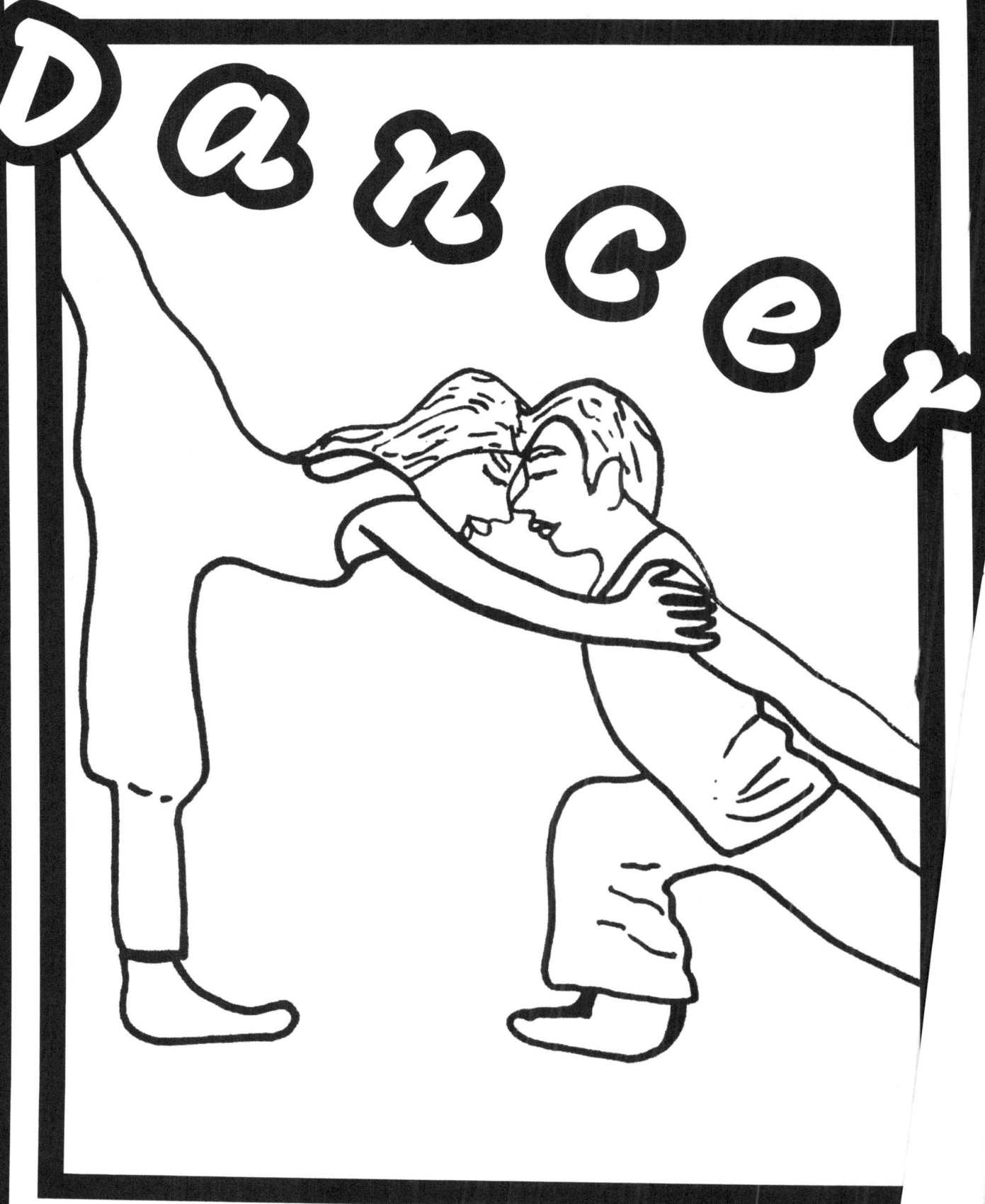

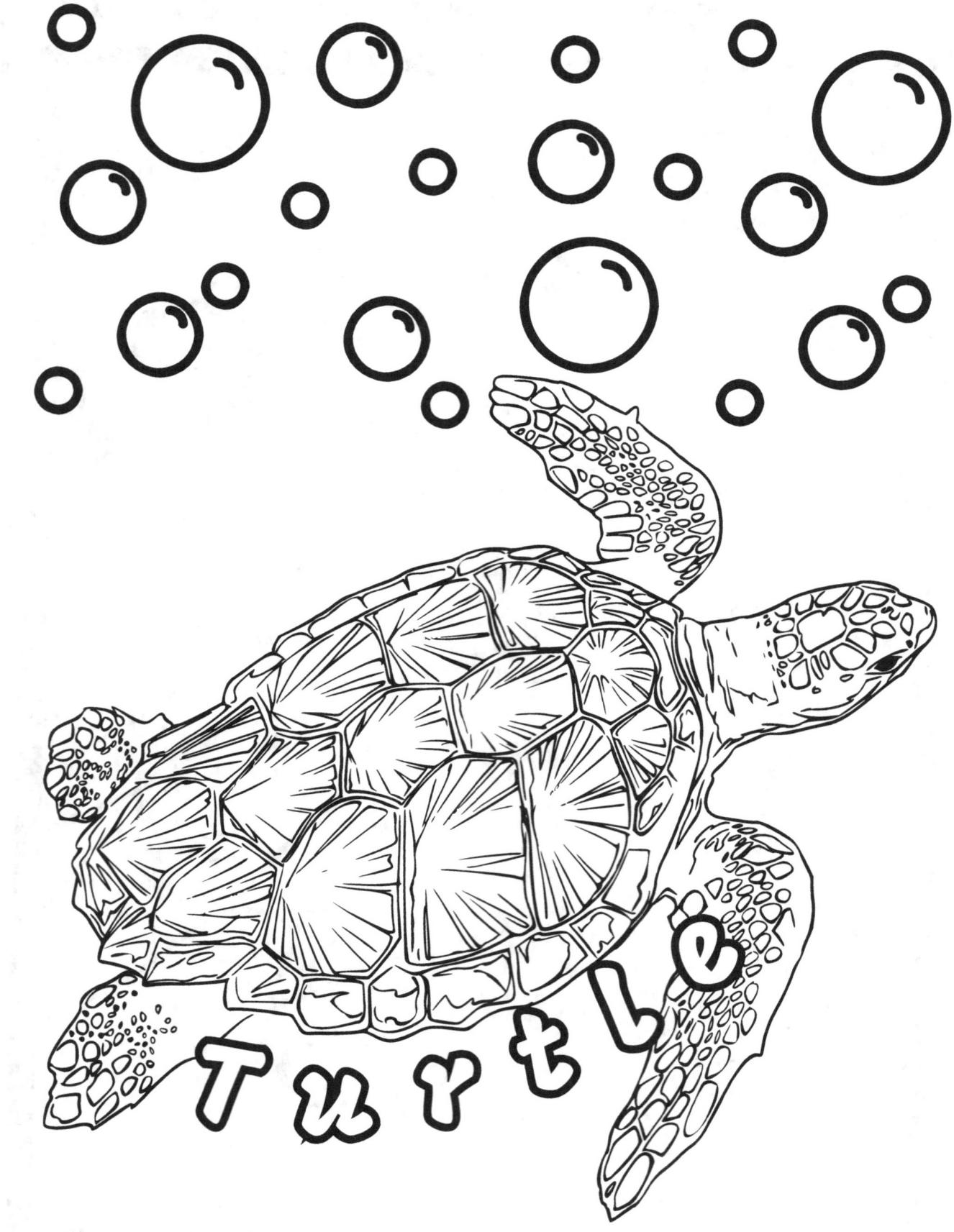

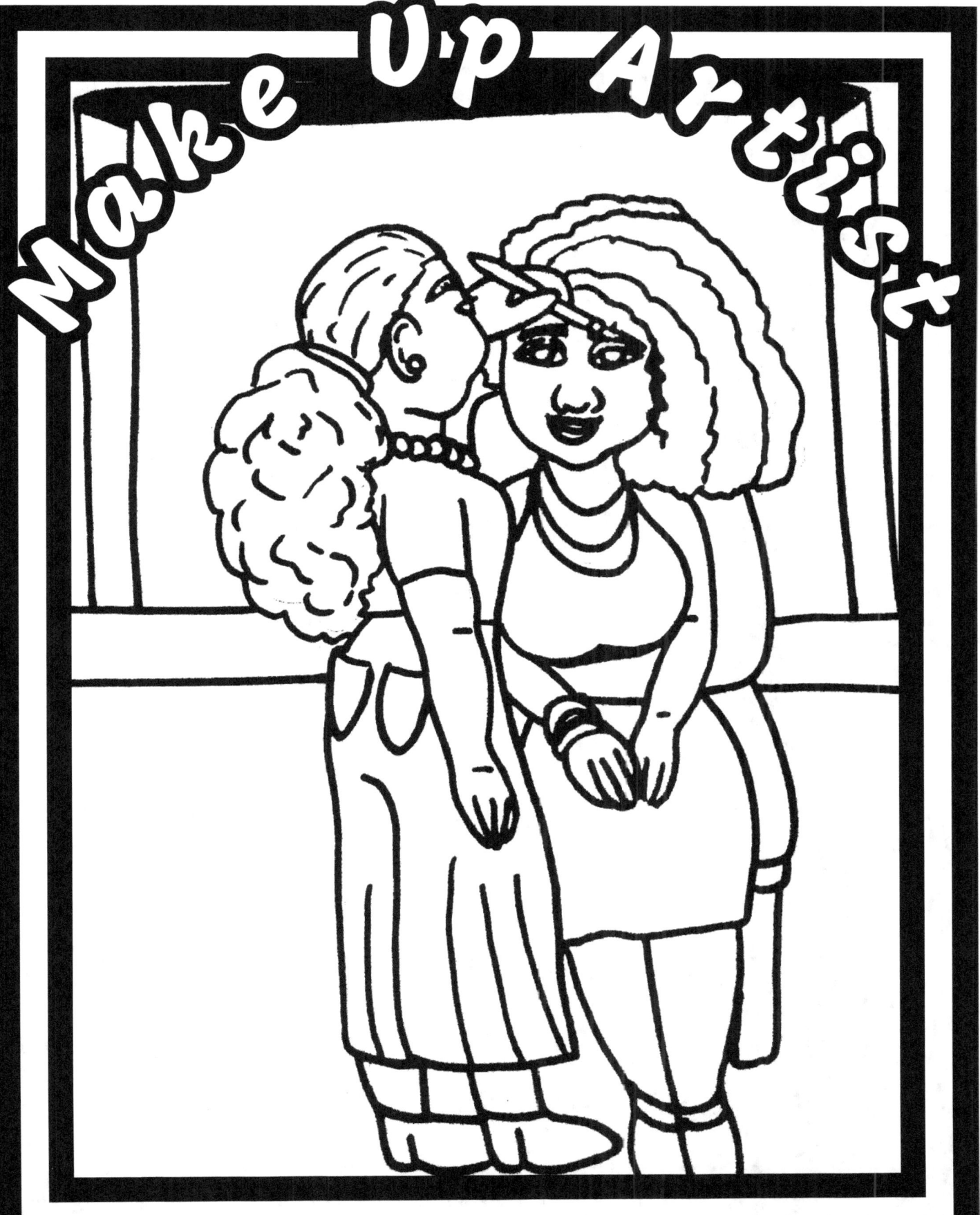

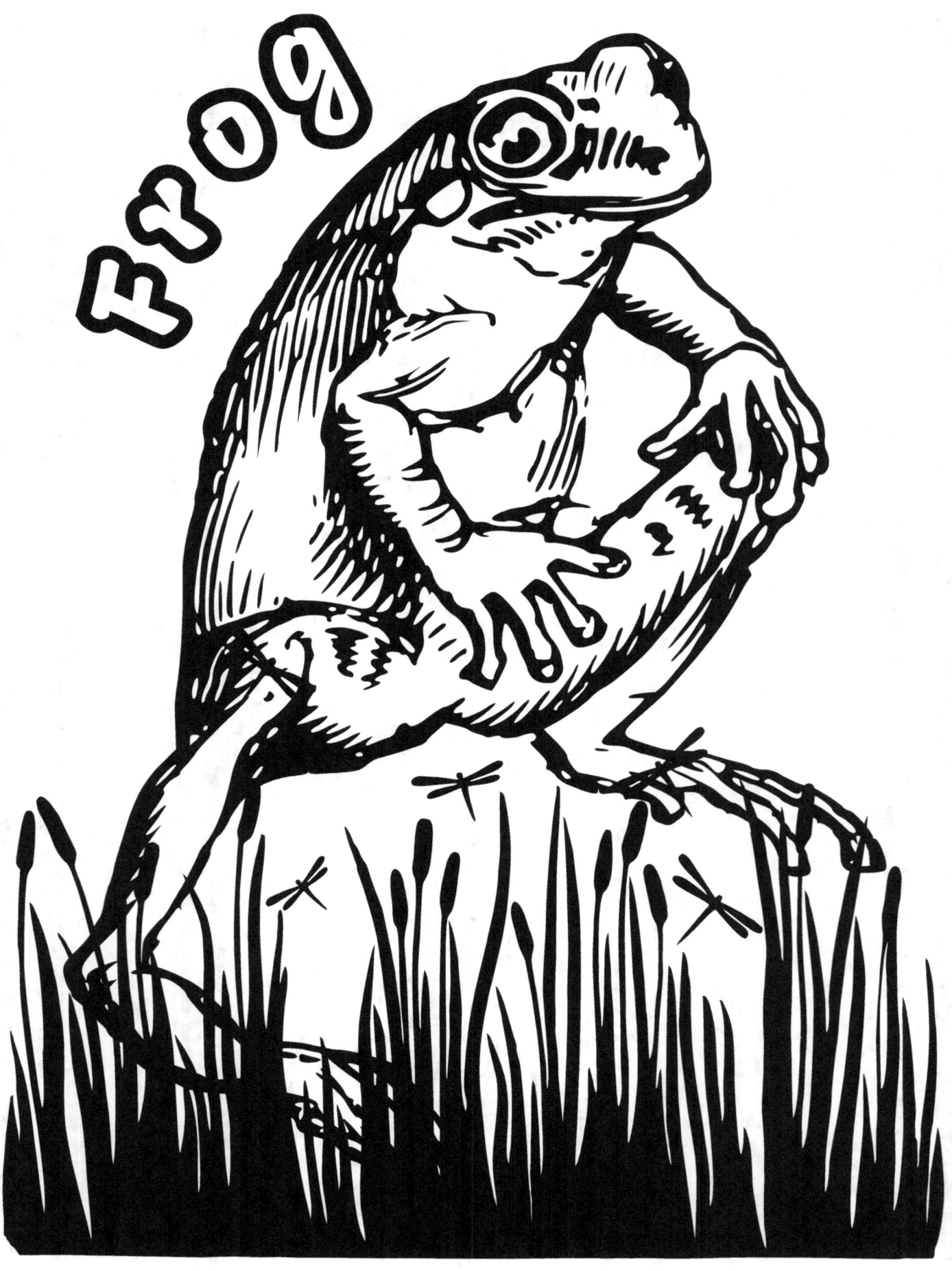

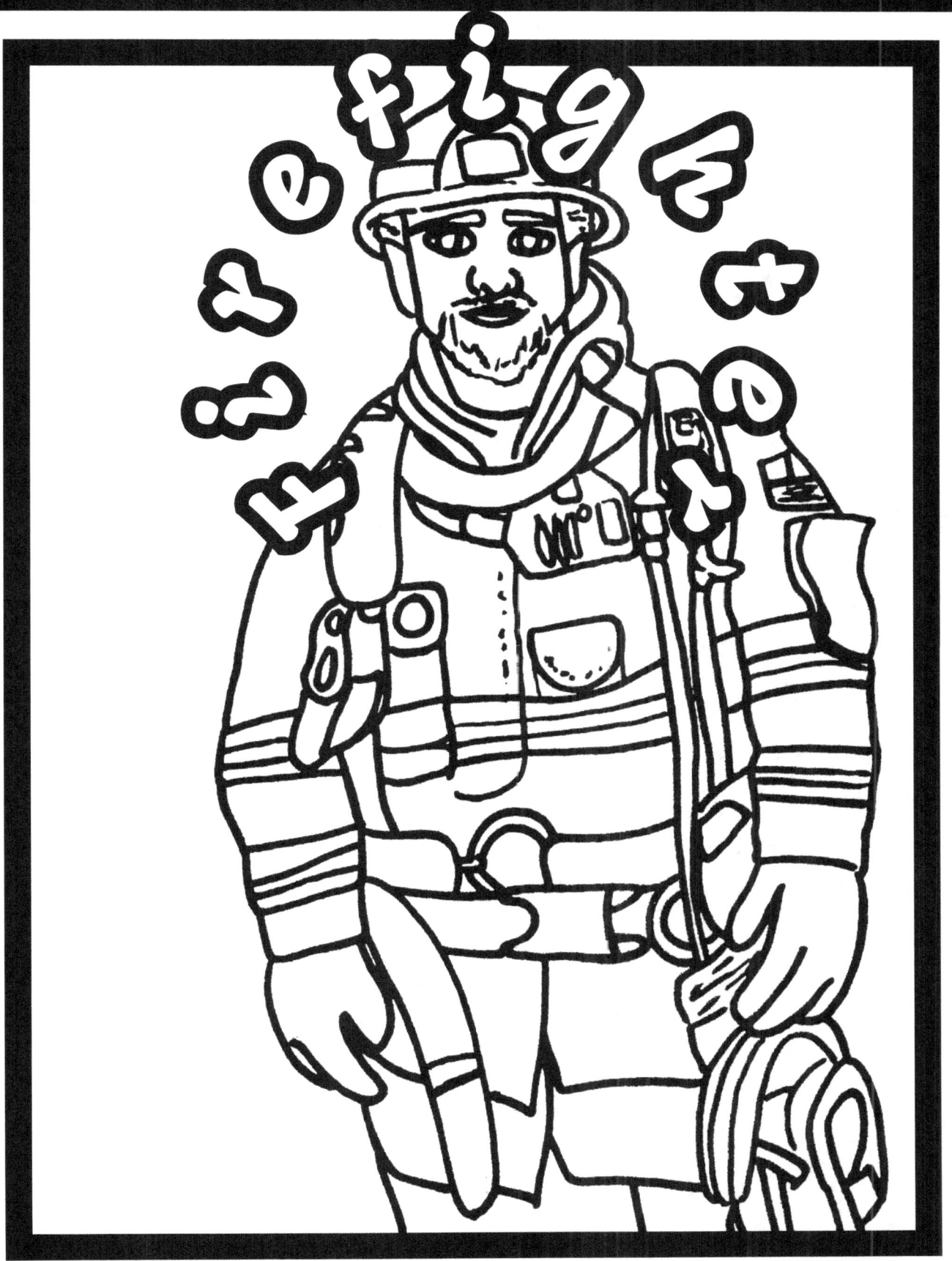

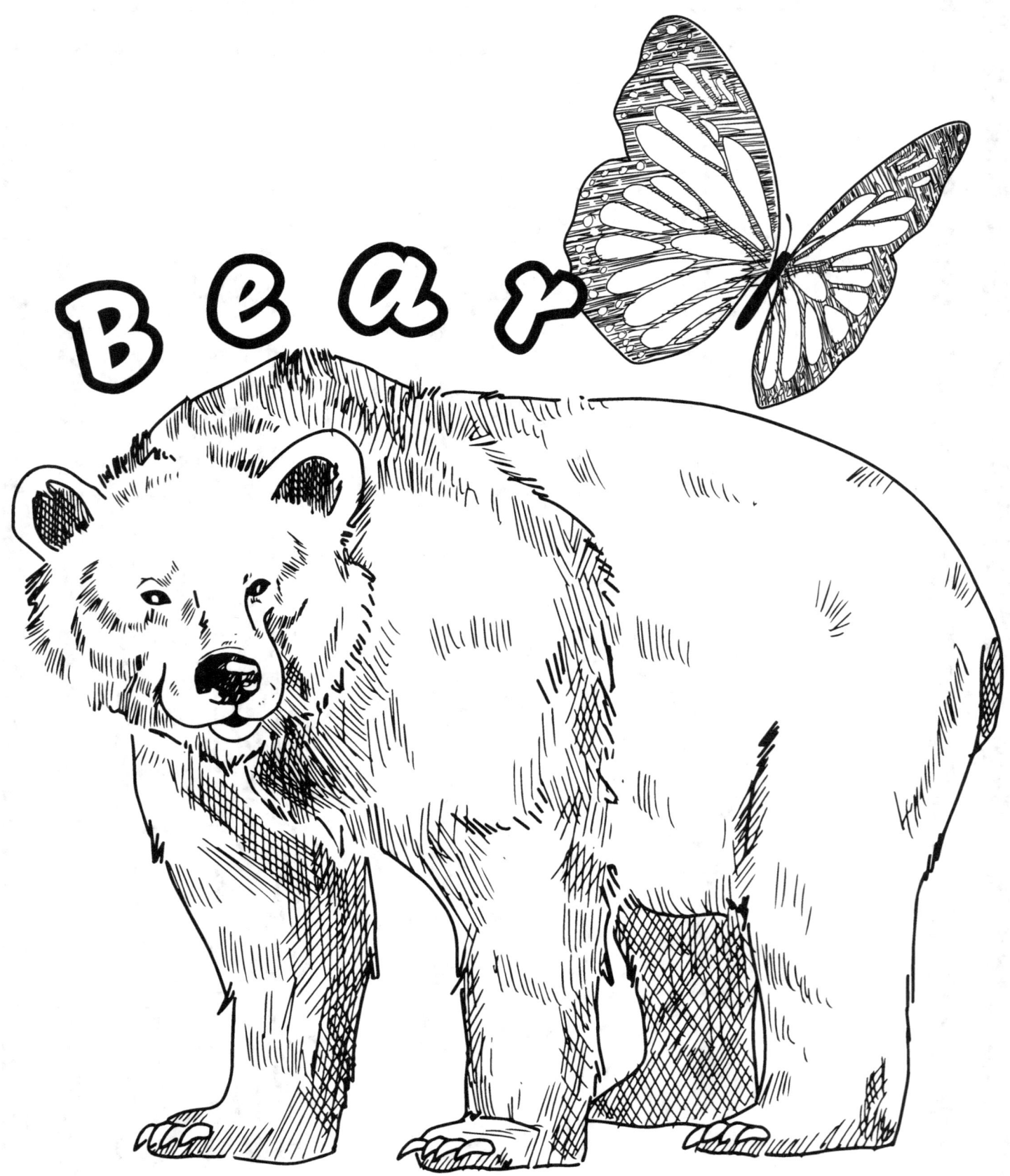

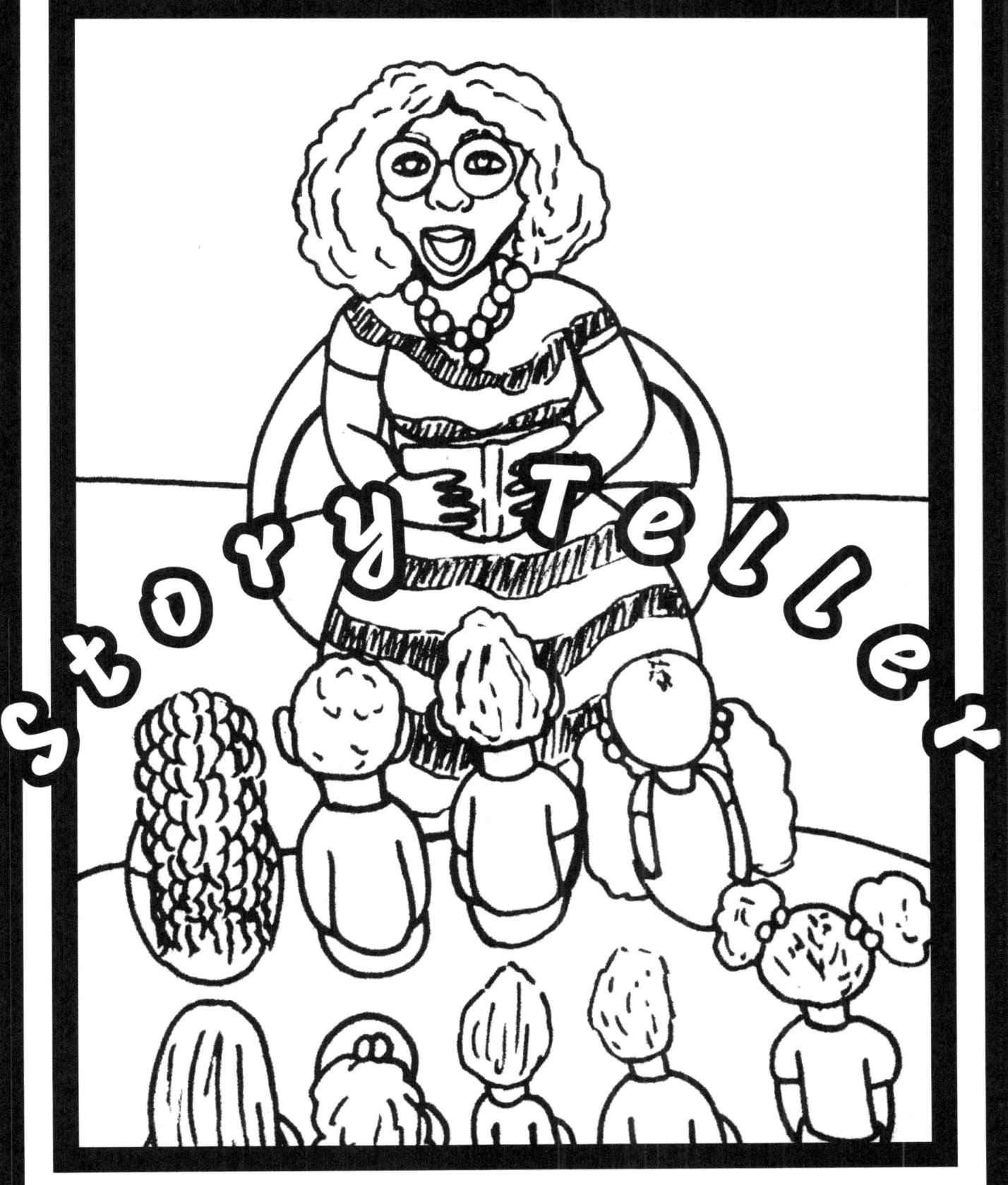

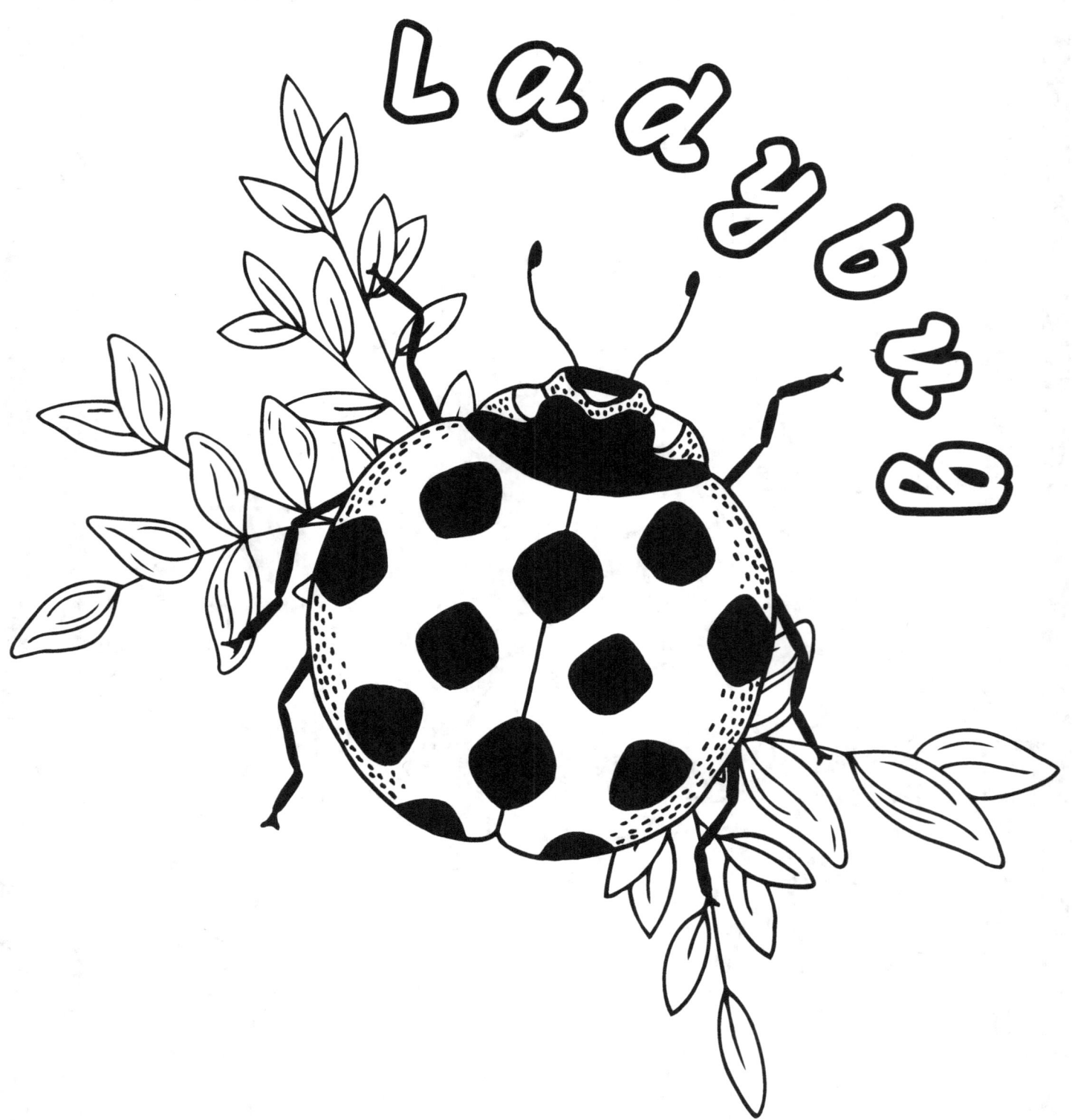

Hairstylist

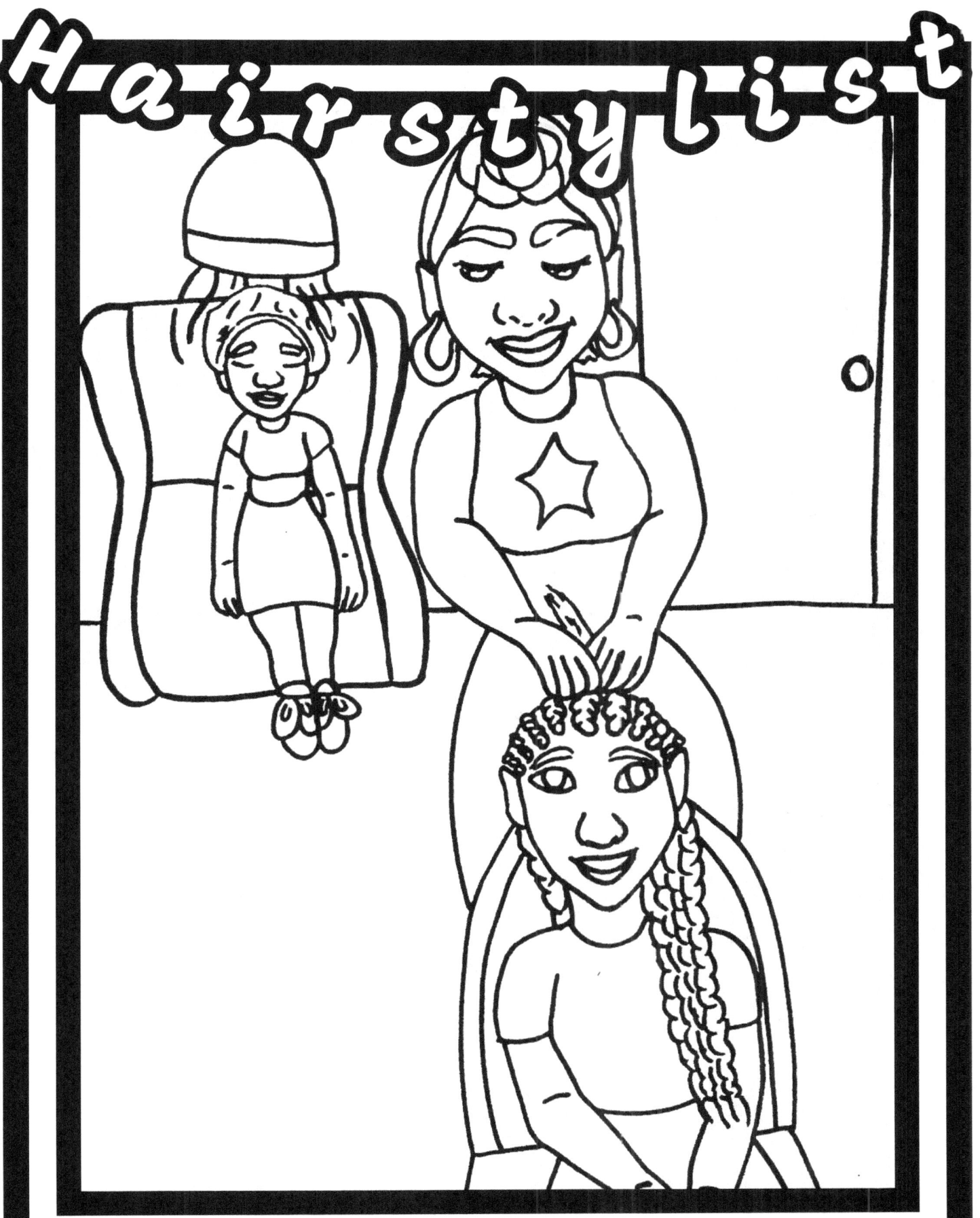

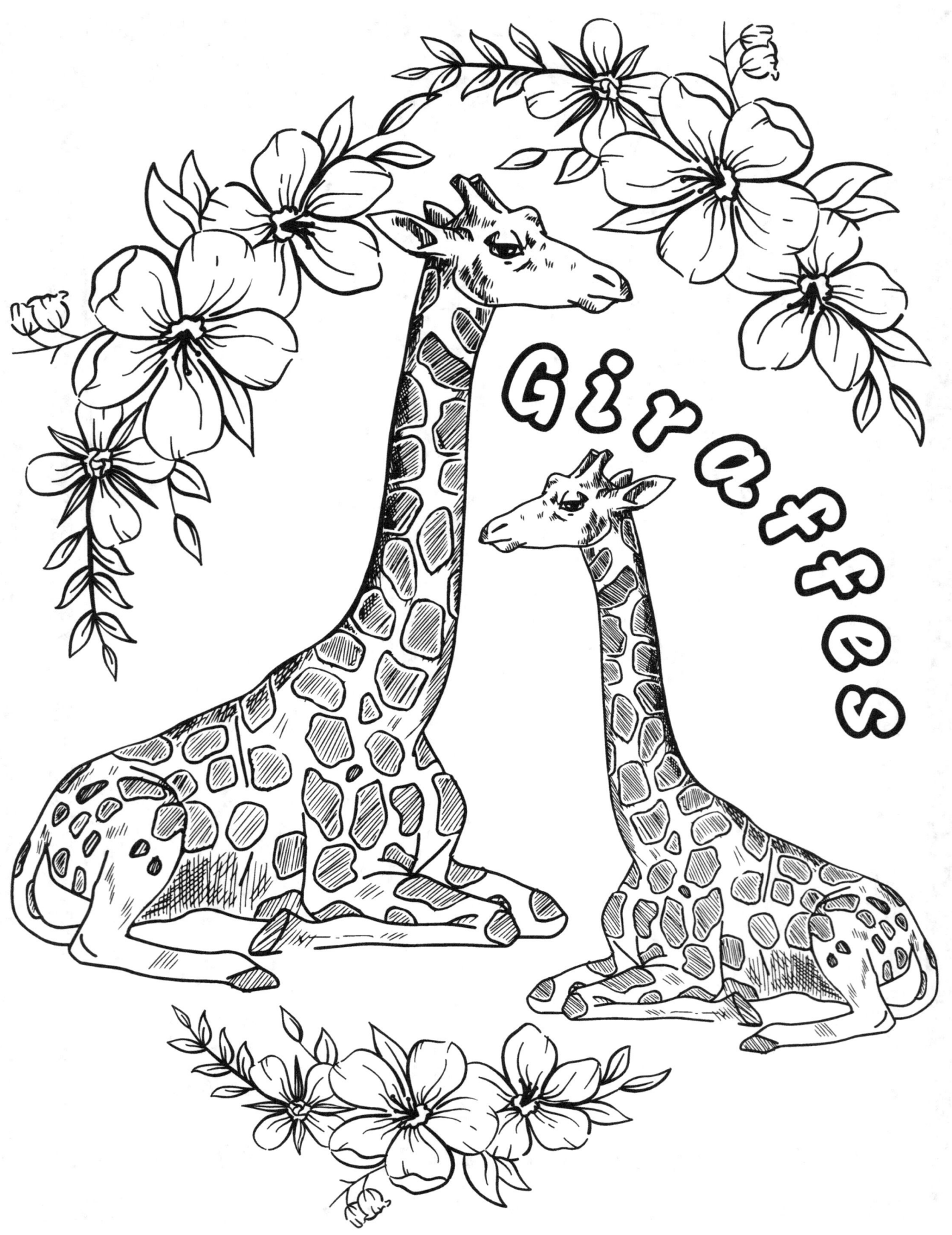

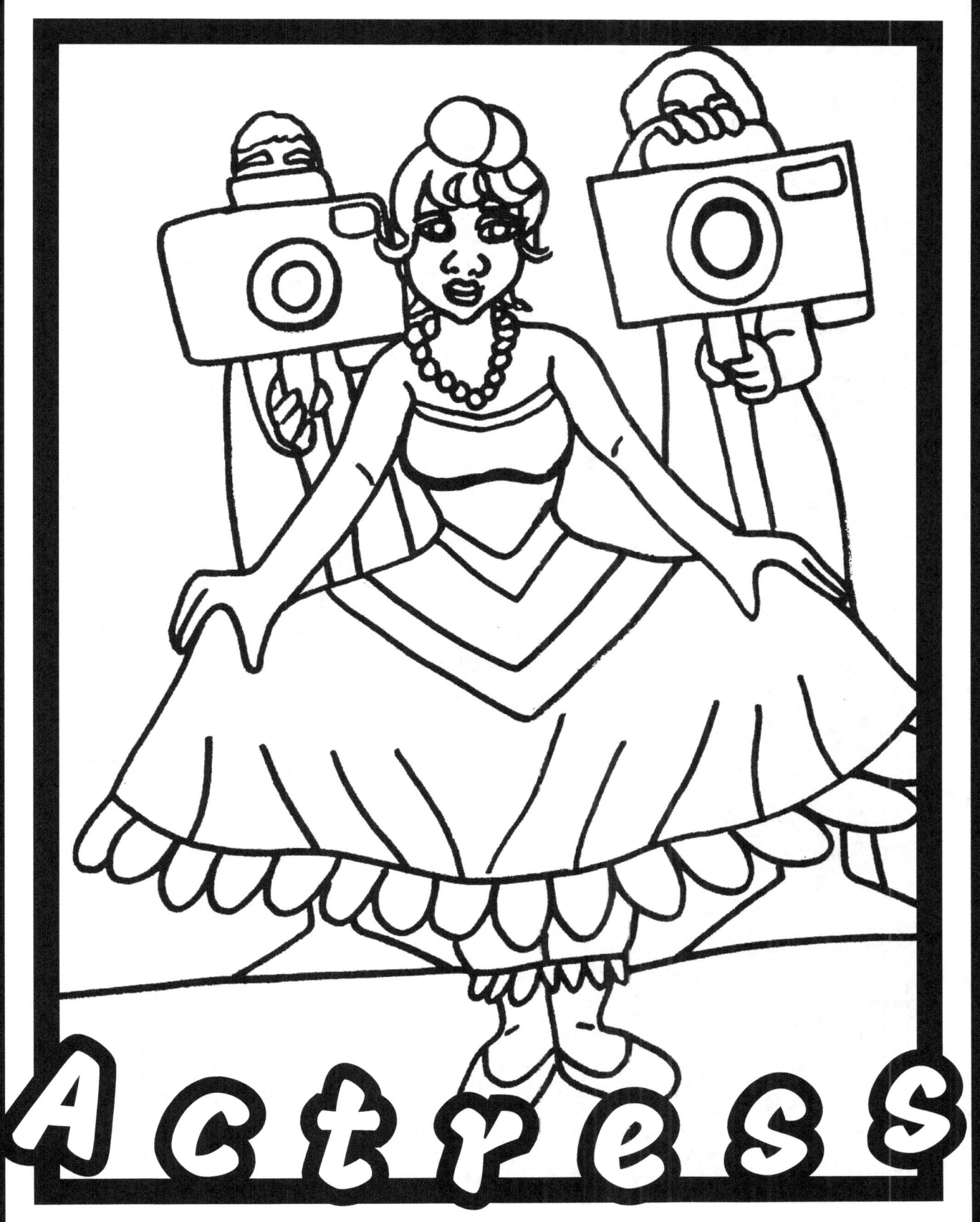

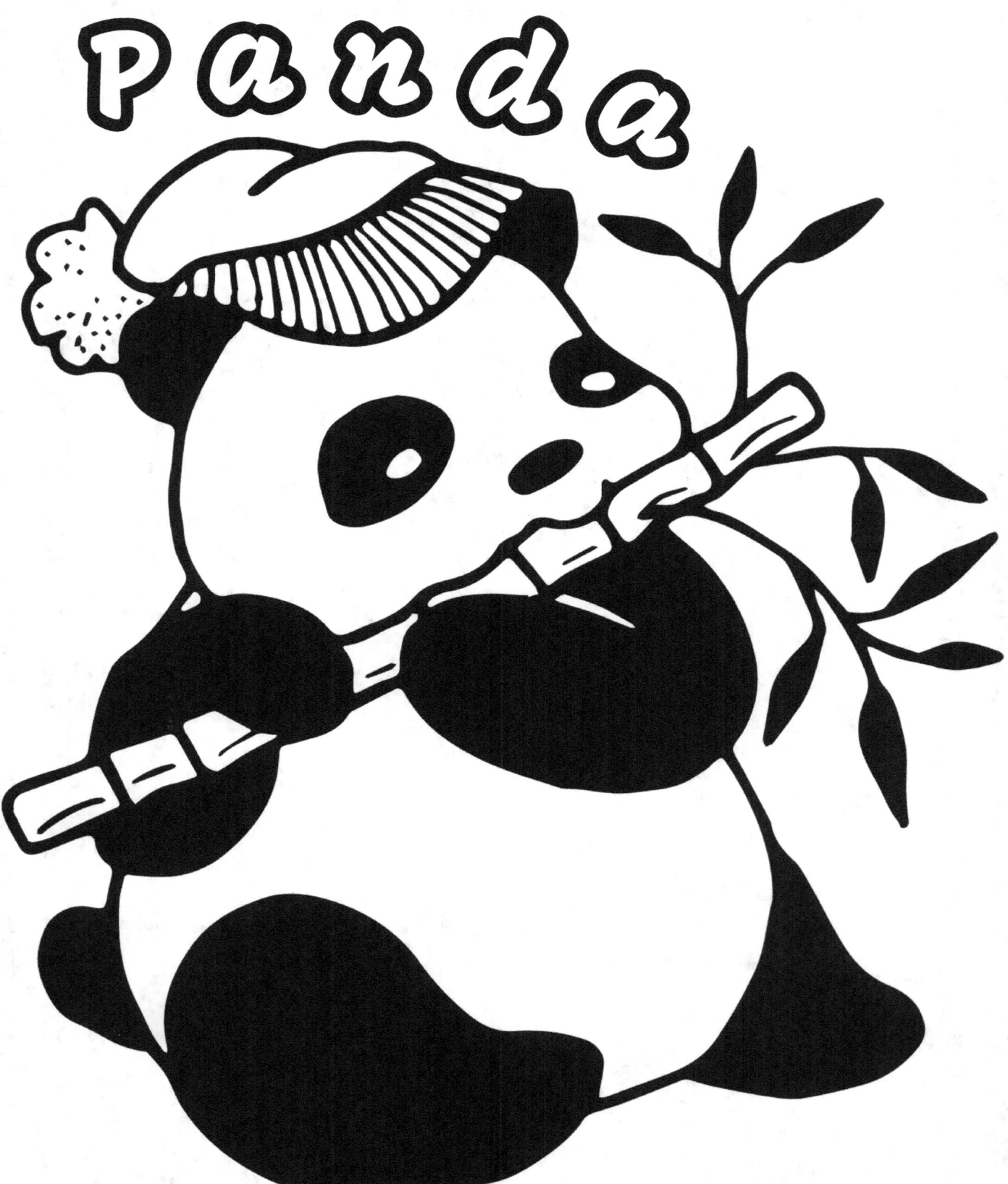

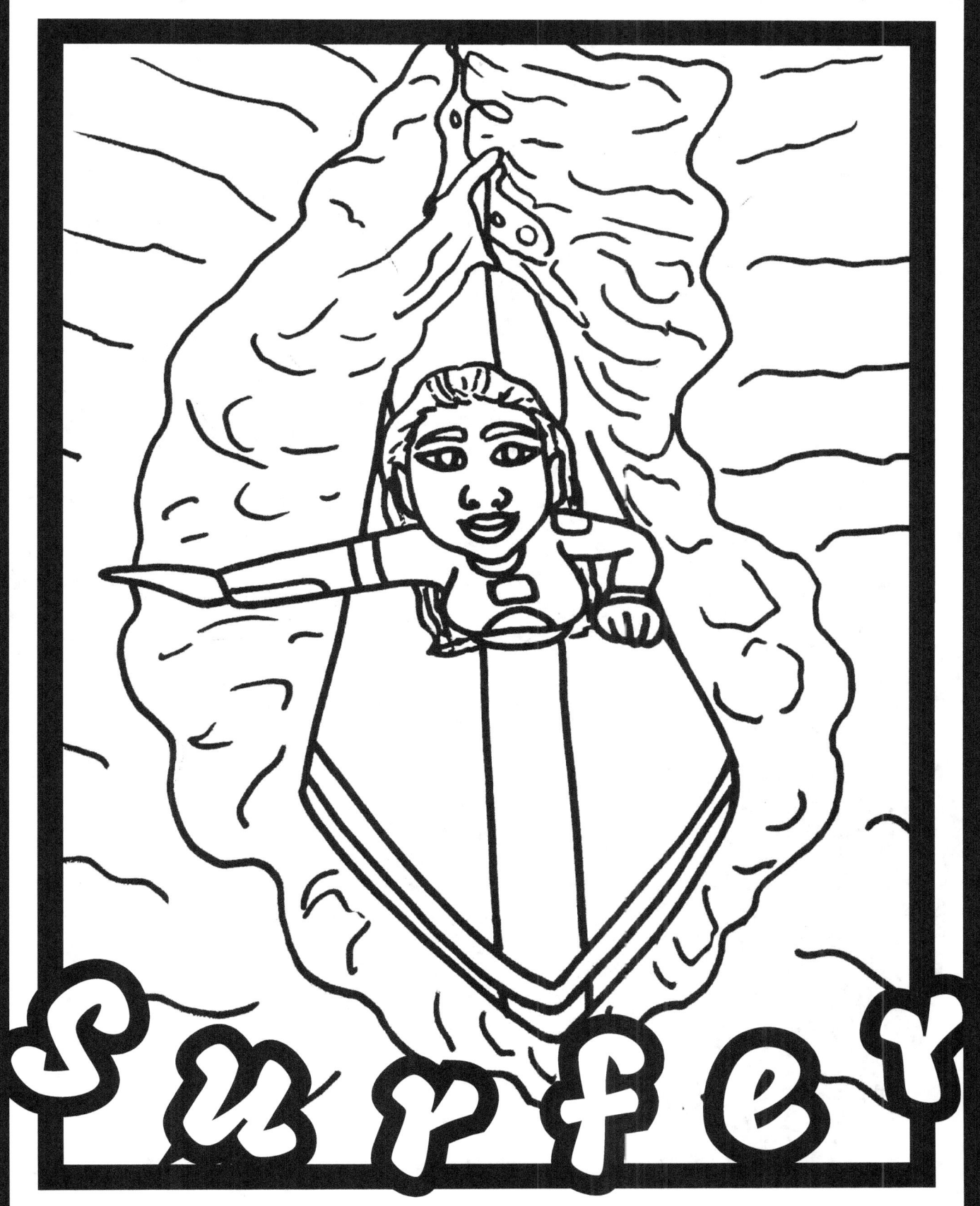

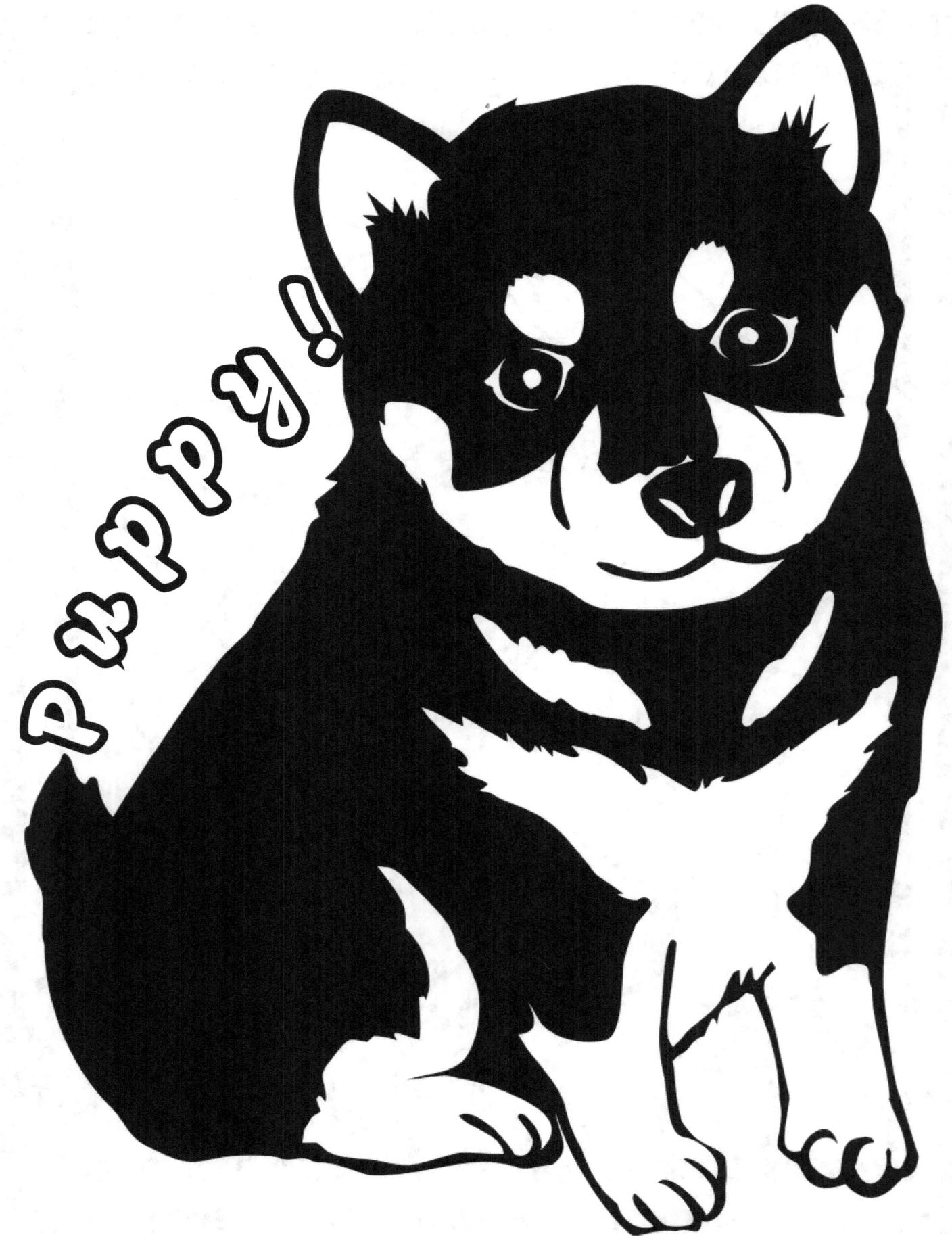

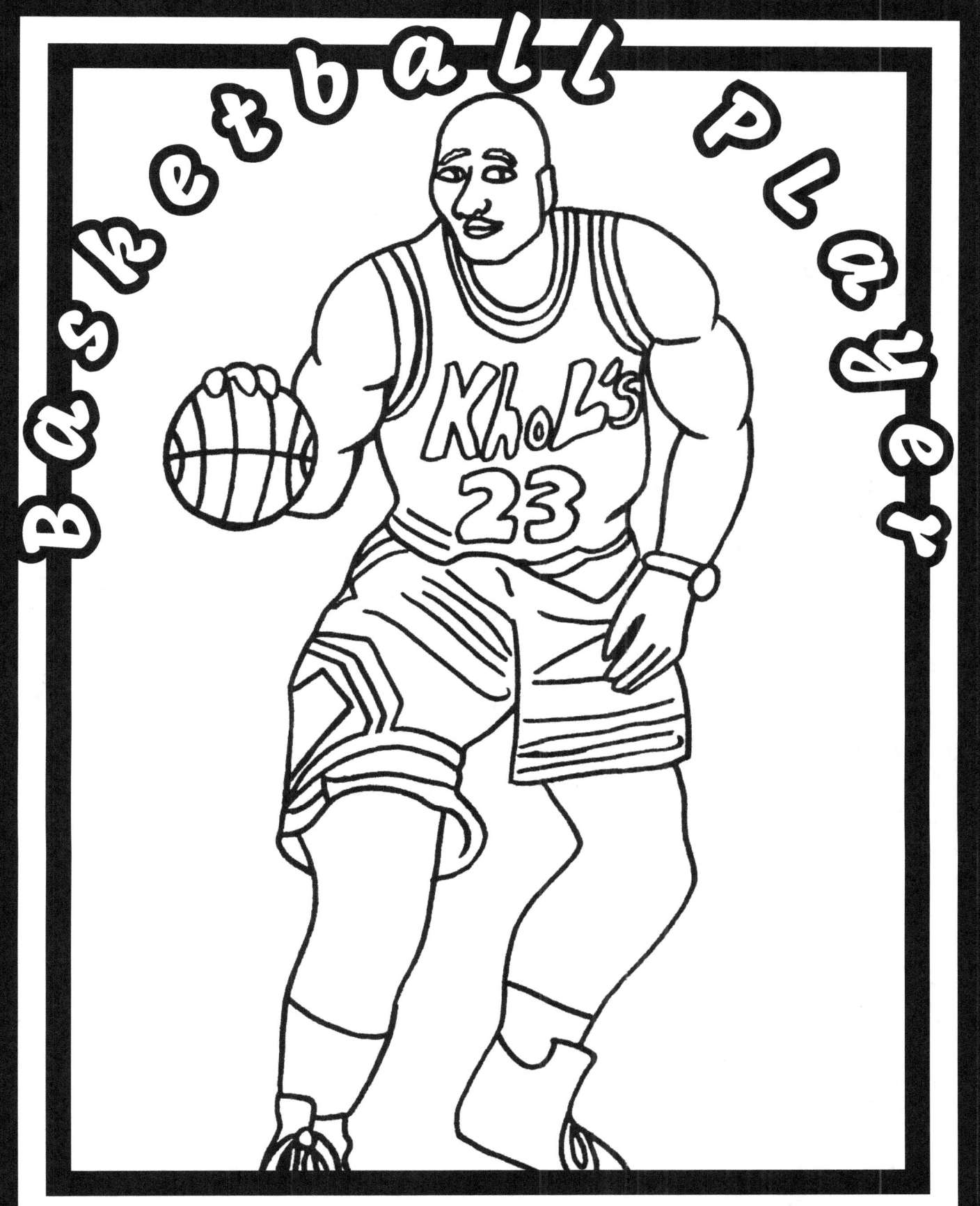

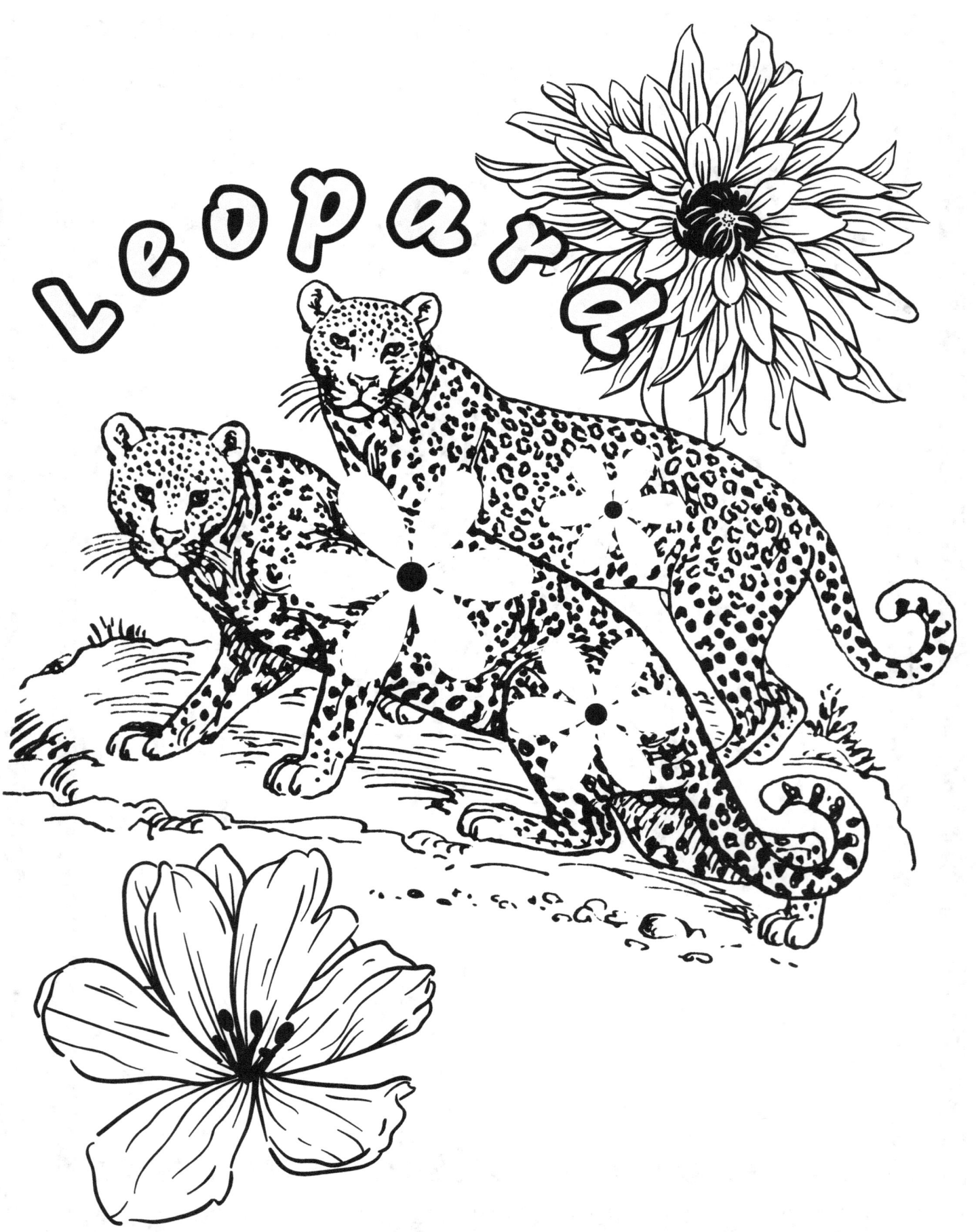

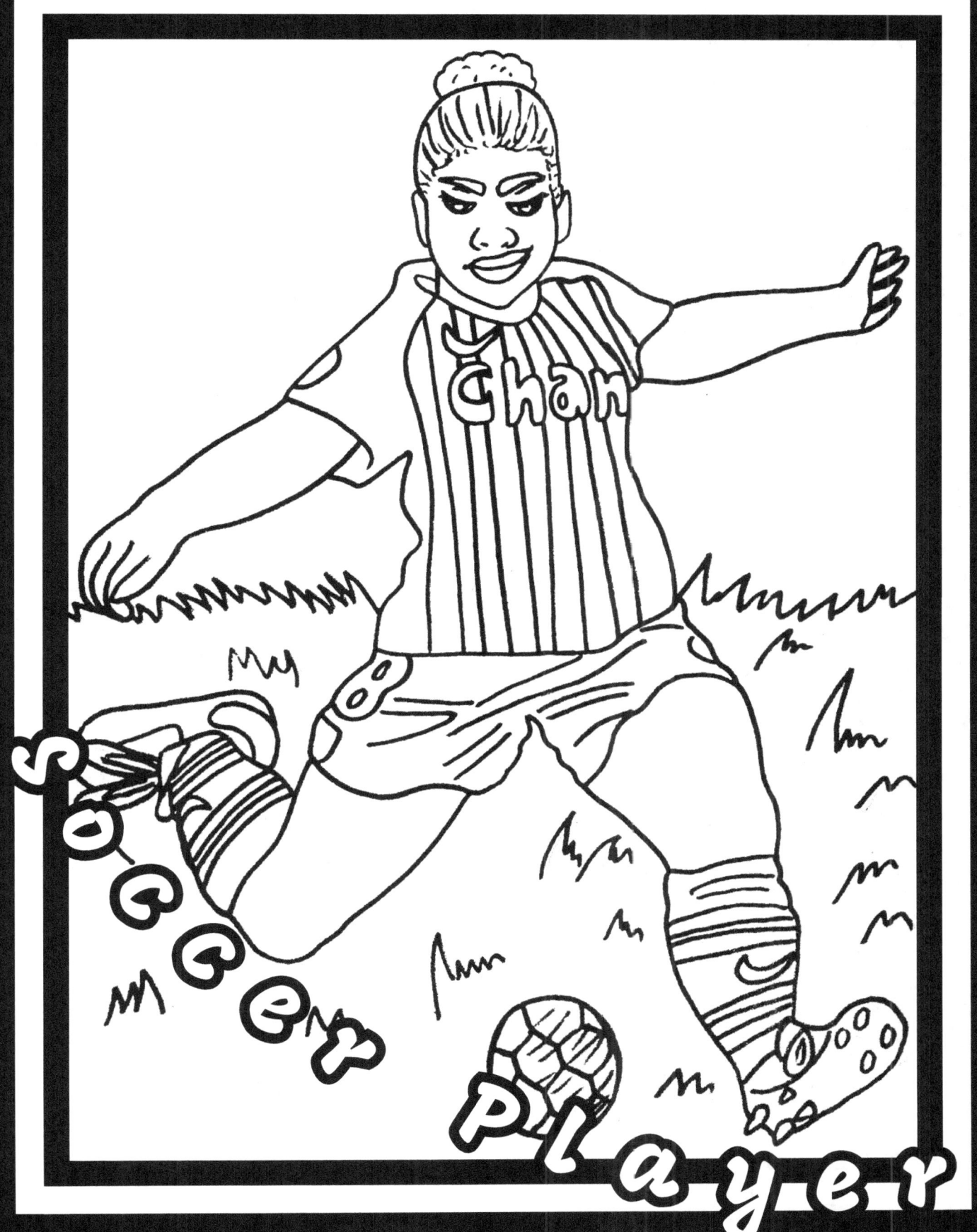

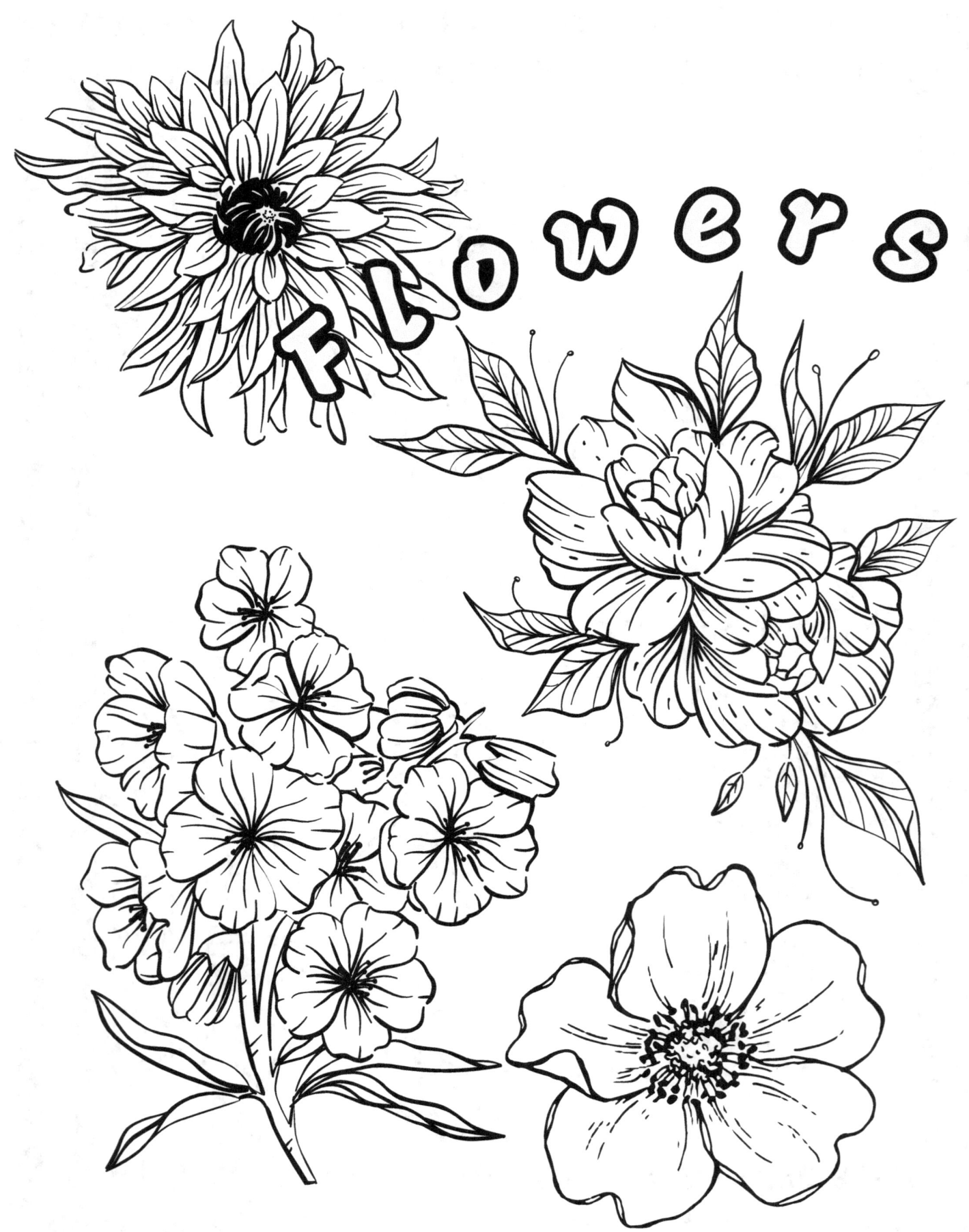

Blacksmith

Dream BIG!
Never Small

Your Extraordinary
Author BTArtist

Dream BIG!

Never Small

Your Extraordinary Author BTArtist

www.ingramcontent.com/pod-product-compliance
Lightning Source LLC
Chambersburg PA
CBHW082159290526
45794CB00008B/3359